The Professor
Grayson Boucher

David Ezra

2018

God bless

The Professor – Grayson Boucher

Plus More NW Sports Stories

By
David Espinoza

E-BookTime, LLC
Montgomery, Alabama

The Professor – Grayson Boucher
Plus More NW Sports Stories

Copyright © 2013 by David Espinoza

All rights reserved. No part of this book may be reproduced or transmitted in any form or by any means, electronic or mechanical, including photocopying, recording, or by any information storage and retrieval system, without permission in writing from the copyright owner.

Library of Congress Control Number: 2013956046

ISBN: 978-1-60862-530-7

First Edition
Published December 2013
E-BookTime, LLC
6598 Pumpkin Road
Montgomery, AL 36108
www.e-booktime.com

Acknowledgements

First and most importantly, I'd like to thank God for the guidance through this inspiring project. I feel blessed to have gotten to know these athletes and their families. It was an honor writing their stories.

My deepest gratitude goes out to these people for the interview time. They also provided photos for me. Thank you!

Grayson Boucher and his parents, Steve and Molly Boucher

Janelle Weiss and her mom, Earleen Weiss

Alex Hurlburt and his parents, Ed and Julie Hurlburt

Avry Holmes and his mom, Cathy Holmes

Brooke Chuhlantseff and her mom, Daniela Chuhlantseff

Daniel Brattain and his parents, Rob and Rhonda Brattain

Brittney Kiser and her parents, Scott and Tara Kiser

Acknowledgements

Noah Torres and his parents, Paul and Sophie Torres

Contributors – Kim Phillips, Willie Freeman, Jeremy Lyon, Latrice Holmes, Kelsey Huber, Nancy Mueller, Jesse Ailstock, and Ron Juarez

Editors – Thanks to my wife, Loni Espinoza – many hours she spent editing with me

Book cover design – Thanks to my son, Jake Espinoza

Source cite tips and back cover photo – Thanks to my son, Matt Espinoza

Contents

Foreword 9

Grayson Boucher "The Professor" Earned His
Streetball Name 11

Janelle Weiss, a Determined Athlete 59

Can't is Not an Option for Alex Hurlburt 78

The Avry Holmes Story, Like Father Like Son 133

Brooke Chuhlantseff Has Olympic Trials Vision 159

Daniel Brattain Has Hurdle Heights to Reach 177

Brittney Kiser, a Swimmer Despite Emotional
Hardship 194

Noah Torres, Nothing Stops this Legend from the
Lake 210

Credits 231

Sources 233

Foreword

By David Espinoza

To have a passion for that one thing you desire in life takes a tremendous amount of hard work, sacrifice, determination, decision making, and support. I'm sure we can create an entire list, but I think you get my point. Some of us want to achieve success – we see the result in our minds. But getting there is a different story. The beauty of discovering the many objectives needed and obstacles to overcome is the challenge. In my opinion, once the objectives are accomplished and the obstacles are worked through, there is a legit chance to reach that goal. If you haven't seen what some people go through in order to become successful, well, let me take you on a journey in the beautiful northwest part of the USA. Allow me to share with you eight stories I call success.

Grayson Boucher "The Professor" Earned His Streetball Name

I'd say that most kids playing sports today want to be tall and strong. Unfortunately, we weren't all made that way. I take great pleasure in sharing an amazing story about a short White skinny kid with blonde hair that inspired many people including myself. He became an overnight sensation signing a contract with the And 1 Mixtape Tour, which was heavily populated with Black players.

And 1 is a shoe company out of Philadelphia that ESPN used to create a streetball TV series. After a six-year run, ESPN did not continue the show. Boucher then signed with Ball Up Streetball – based in Los Angeles, California.

He toured all over the world playing basketball in front of thousands. He even landed a part as an extra in the movie *Semi-Pro* with Woody Harrelson and Will Ferrell. His big jump to the big screen was a lead role in the movie *Ball Don't Lie,* featuring Rosanne Arquette, Nick Cannon, Ludacris, and Kim Hidalgo. I had the opportunity to watch this movie at the 2008 Seattle Film Festival – great movie.

Grayson Boucher grew up in Keizer, Oregon, but was born in Salem, Oregon, at Salem General Hospital in 1984. Salem and Keizer sit right next to each other on the map. He is the son of Steve and Molly. He also has a brother, Landon, who he's very close to.

At that time Steve was working for Boucher Jewelers – a family-owned business. Molly was selling shoes at a local store. They now are co-owners of Boucher Jewelers.

Grayson came from a middle-income-class family. The neighborhood was safe and stable. His parents were over protective of him and his brother. Molly figures they should take good care of both their boys until someday two nice girls might take over the duties.

"Molly would drive the boys to school and back every day. And the school was only three blocks away! We really wanted our boys to be safe," Steve laughs.

Steve played basketball when he was in high school, and Molly played some church league. After high school, Steve played city league basketball with a group of guys. It was then (at three years old) that Grayson was introduced to the game of basketball. He really enjoyed watching the games his dad played in. Sitting on the bench, he would intensely observe the game – constantly learning different things.

"My dad inspired me to start loving the game of basketball – I was trying to be like Dad, you know?" Grayson expressed.

Most of the kids that went to the games ran around like any normal kid would, but there was something about Grayson that identified him as unique. Basketball seemed to be the game that caught his attention.

His dad remembers purchasing a Larry Bird hoop for indoor shooting. Grayson took it to heart and started shooting baskets every day on it. He had a natural instinct to hit the basket. With practice he became better each day.

Grayson Boucher "The Professor" Earned His Streetball Name

Grayson's childhood environment was being around his cousins most of the time, Brent and Kristy, and their parents, Ron Boucher and Deena Brottingham. The other cousins are, Amber, Brycen, and Shelby – their parents, Jeff and Dephne Boucher. They got together often. It seemed like every weekend he wanted to go over to the cousins' house. He also had a few neighborhood friends, but only because they had something to do with basketball. Two friends that were not related to Grayson were Nick Bauer and Ernie Sturzinger.

His parents never wanted him to be anything other than what he wanted to be. They always wondered what he would become in the future. He was a kid that was always trying to develop his own style. He was a huge Michael Jackson fan growing up – learned all of Michael's dance moves close to perfection. This young man was also attentive on what kind of clothes to wear. He had to have that style that made him look good.

Basketball-card collecting was a hobby he enjoyed. Most kids were into that in the 1990s – Becket, Fleer etc. Trading cards with friends and looking around at card shops was an exciting adventure for the young kids.

There were a few things Grayson did away from basketball but he mostly had that drive to perfect his ball handling and shooting as a youngster. His parents thought he could be an outstanding long-distant runner. In 1994 they entered him in the annual running event called the Awesome 3000 – thousands of kids from many grade schools in the Salem/Keizer area competed in this race. Of course the program tries to teach kids that everyone's a winner. For the Bouchers there was only one winner, they wanted Grayson to win – it was important. He won the race with flying colors. He was a short skinny blonde kid and definitely built like a runner.

Molly tried introducing her son to other things. She signed him up for tennis lessons, golf lessons, and swimming lessons. She even tried signing him up for Boy Scouts.

"Believe it or not, I remember sending him to babysitting school. We just wanted him to try different things. But it seems like no matter what we introduced him to, he would always go back to basketball. That was his passion," Molly said.

Grayson attended Kennedy Elementary School first through third grade, Gubser Elementary fourth through fifth, and Whiteaker Middle School sixth through eighth.

During the early school days, Grayson got along very well with his peers. He was known as the class clown. He was a showoff type of kid that made people laugh. He could impersonate just about anyone he knew – a teacher, a friend, or a coach. He seemed to have that skill.

Oh, and let's not talk about grades, because he'll be the first to admit that he just did enough to get by. He did not put in the effort academically that he was capable of. Grayson was actually a very bright kid – studying just wasn't his bag at the time.

"I wish I could take those moments back. Now that I'm grown up I regret doing school the wrong way – just getting by. Education is really important. I focused on basketball all the time. For a lot of kids it won't turn out like it did for me. I was fortunate to have made the And 1 Mixtape Tour," Grayson said.

Grayson never had issues with anyone as a young kid. But he does remember one instance that scared the lights out of him. He remembers Shiloh Rowland, a high school teenager. As a middle-school kid, Grayson was walking down the street one day spitting toward the street. Shiloh drove by with his truck and thought he saw the spit wad hit his truck. Naturally he pulls over in front of Grayson.

"Why are you spitting at my truck!" Shiloh yelled.

Grayson was terrified of this big guy that was yelling at him all the way home. This was probably the only moment that he thought of himself as being bullied.

"I'm sure Shiloh was just playing around with me at the time, but it sure scared the daylights out of me – ha-ha!" Grayson laughs.

To be heavily involved in basketball at a young age is an understatement. His dad, Steve, coached Grayson's KYBA team (Keizer Youth Basketball Association). It's like a pee-wee basketball league. The kids were third and fourth graders when they started this league. This was a big deal to the entire family. They would attend the McNary High School games, and at half-time the KYBA kids played in front of a big crowd. To Grayson, being in the spotlight and scoring baskets was an amazing experience – he really enjoyed that.

"I owe my parents so much. They got me gym memberships, took me to camps, put in a driveway hoop, paid for private ball-handling lessons, bought me sneakers, and many other things. My dad was always a fan of the Portland Trailblazers and still is. He would take me to some of the games. I'm blessed to have such amazing parents that took good care of me and my brother Landon," Grayson said.

His parents never missed anything he was a part of. They always tried to instill good values in him. They wanted him to become a good person and to take everything serious.

"Everything you do should be important," Steve said.

Molly drove Grayson all over the state for all sorts of basketball tournaments, contests, tryouts, etc. And Steve would shake his head up and down strongly.

"Life is like a big competition. I expected Grayson to work hard at anything he did. It was easy for me, because Grayson is a 'do-gooder' type of kid – like my wife says. He always wants to do what's right. We've always tried to put both of our kids in a position where they could have the best opportunity," Steve said.

Grayson has overcome a few obstacles in his life as a young kid. He was born with hip dysplasia. This condition affects the hip ball, the socket of the joint, or both. There is treatment for this condition. The cause is not really known. Genetics play a role but not the direct cause.
Grayson worked through this condition with needed treatment. As the years passed he improved and was able to walk normal. Grayson then became a great runner as mentioned previously.
When Grayson was in the fifth grade he was always one of the skinniest and shortest players on any team. This was one of his major obstacles. His dad went through the same thing when he was growing up. There were so many uncomfortable situations he had to deal with. He worried about getting weighed in front of students, height measurement, and some harsh jokes now and then.
There was a time that Grayson jumped off of a flight of steps. I'd say about ten feet high or so (that's the height of

the rim – interesting). When he landed, the cartilage in his vertebra compressed so much that he was injured for a few weeks – he had to sit out for several games. He fought through the pain and worked his way back into the lineup.

Kids do things sometimes not realizing that the adventure could result in a serious injury. But although Grayson had severe pain in is back for weeks, it was more painful for him to sit out and watch his team play from the bench.

As time passed he eventually healed and was back in business – working hard on the basketball floor. He'd practice anywhere, the drive-way hoop or wherever he could find a game.

"I was in the fifth grade when I started realizing that I had a gift of handling the basketball. I never really thought about how good I was becoming. I would hear positive comments from other players and parents," Grayson said.

Sometimes during tournaments Grayson would play up one grade. He was playing in a fifth-grade tournament as a fourth grader. In a game against West Salem, the Celts were trailing. The fourth quarter arrived and Grayson took over. He managed to score 24 points in the fourth quarter and hit a buzzer-beater game-winning shot! The crowd went wild! He's the kind of player that would hit a clutch shot at the end of a game.

He loved the game of basketball, but because of the time spent playing the game and practicing, he sometimes felt like he was missing out on other things. Things like having a girlfriend, or participating in other school activities – maybe like a school dance. He never thought about making some of those things happen. But you could certainly find him playing pick-up basketball somewhere.

"I'd see some of my friends with girlfriends. I never had a girlfriend all through my school days. Sometimes I felt sad that I didn't do some of those things in school," Grayson said.

One year, Grayson was attending the Pro-Classic Camp. This was a camp that was held every year at Willamette University in Salem, Oregon. Gordy James was the director and head men's basketball coach of the university at the time.

It was at this camp that Grayson met Rodney Howard, a former Oregon State Beaver who played point guard in college. In fact, Rodney is a former teammate of Gary Payton. Gary was OSU's leading scorer while playing there – he continued his career in the NBA.

Grayson found out that Rodney was a personal trainer – specializing in ball-handling techniques and other skills. Grayson talked to his parents about Rodney. Steve and Molly were the type of parents that would do anything to feed their son's passion. They instantly hired Rodney to work with Grayson.

"Rodney taught me so many things. He helped me make my crossover what it is today. He perfected that move within my capabilities. People actually started watching me and making comments on the way I handled the ball," Grayson said.

While Grayson was attending Whiteaker Middle School, he joined a tournament team called the Keizer Celts A Team. The team was coached by Ernie Sturzinger. His son, Eric, was competing for playing time with Grayson – they were both point guards. Sometimes when parents are coaches, issues arise with players on the team or with parents. It's not always an easy thing to deal with for either side. Grayson didn't feel like his style was fitting to what this team wanted. He was struggling with the whole situation.

Keizer had another team called the Keizer Celts B-Plus Team. Kevin Taylor coached that team. The Bouchers found out that there was an opening for one more player to join. At that time Grayson wanted to do more for any team he played with. The problem was that not all coaches liked his style of play. Kevin was a coach that knew Grayson's style of play and actually liked it.

Becoming part of the Keizer Celt's B-Plus Team was a good move for him. This team played in many A-team tournaments. The competition was just as good. Grayson had the green light to play basketball with his flashy style – he helped this team win games against A teams from all over the state.

By the time he was a freshman in high school, his game had developed more and his skills were very noticeable. How does a kid prepare for high school basketball? For Grayson, he didn't realize he had been doing that all along.

"Working with Rodney helped improve my ball-handling skills to another level. But because I loved the game so much, I think that alone prepared me. I just didn't realize it," Grayson said.

The result was the same for every camp he attended. Grayson received an all-around award for competitions, whether it was a free-shot competition or a hotshot competition. At the Pro-Classic Camp he set a record for the hotshot competition. This competition allowed a shooter to take shots from different spots around the key in a limited time. This camp usually had hundreds of athletes attending several sessions. There were day campers and overnight campers. They would use the Willamette University campus dorms.

It's such a blessing for kids to have this opportunity – Grayson was one of those kids. To him it was a week of paradise in basketball heaven.

At the OSU Eddie Payne Camp, he won every competition they had. There was at least five during the week session. That takes some doing – he had that natural ability to do well under pressure. It all made sense with the hours of practice he had put in.

During his freshman year at McNary High School he played point guard. The freshman coach was Kevin Taylor. The highlight game had to be the one where he scored 30 points against North Salem High School. McNary played in the Valley League, which at the time was 4A – the big-school's league. Grayson shot 8 for 8 from 3-point land.

Entering his sophomore year he played under Jim Litchfield. Jim was a fundamental-style coach – a disciplined style of basketball. Grayson had a flashy style of play. This was an opportunity for Grayson to learn more about different aspects of the game – very educational. Larry Gahr was the head coach for the varsity boys' team and ran the McNary Basketball Program. Larry ran a program that used a lot of plays on the offensive end. His program was one that prepared kids for college basketball.

The big plus about Larry was that he had "study tables" for athletes that struggled academically. It's so important for kids to make the grades – with the ultimate goal of helping the team at the same time.

Grayson admits that he didn't understand defense too well. He was an offensive threat, but at McNary, slow-down offense and defense were more important to the coaches. Don't get me wrong, fast breaks were executed now and then if an absolute opportunity arose.

This caused some tension between the coaches, player, and parents. Grayson knew he had to work harder at defense, but his struggles became more difficult with the slow-down style of play. He was a kid that always did what the coaches asked – he respected that. Keeping feelings inside was not easy for him but he managed to get by.

At McNary, Grayson's parents didn't feel like the attention was focused on Grayson's career as a point guard. The problem (which not many schools had) was that the team had three point guards that could play excellent defense. In my opinion, Grayson's offensive skills would surpass most of them. Brian Zielinski, Chad Harms, and Josh Erickson. These guys could all play amazing defense, but lacked a little on offensive skills, with the acceptation of Josh Erickson. Josh could play both very well, but lacked in height – he was short just like Grayson. So naturally during his sophomore year on the JV team, Josh played the point-guard and Grayson played the wing position.

"We just didn't feel like McNary had any confidence in Grayson. We always supported McNary anyway we could. Grayson's defense was picking up and he worked hard to improve during the off-season. Grayson never felt the way I did, it was mostly me," Steve said.

Playing under Jim Litchfield as a junior on JV was not easy for Grayson, but like his mom said, he was a "do-gooder." He always wanted to do what was right – he always did what the coaches asked of him and respected their decisions on the court. Grayson appreciated the fact that Jim gave him the playing time to help him improve his game. As a young sophomore he understood and respected that the coach was trying to win games by utilizing the strongest team environment.

There was a game that Grayson was called for a technical foul. A bigger kid from the opposing team was guarding him. The kid said something to him – possible trash talk. Grayson slammed the ball down on the court and the referee gave him a technical foul. The frustrations through the season could have caused this breakdown.

"My mom started crying. She was really embarrassed. She was not only worried about me, but also about keeping a good image and all," Grayson said.

In high school Grayson had made new friends. Most of these kids played basketball at the Courthouse Athletic Club or at The Hoop (a basketball facility) just about every day. During football and track seasons, he'd hit the gym after school – any opportunity he had. Some of his closer friends were, Matt Espinoza, Jake Espinoza, Jared Wick, Robbie Wood, Nick Bauer, and Jeremiah Dominguez.

Grayson was getting ready for his junior year. He was placed on the JV team for the summer league. Rumors heard were hints that Grayson might not be the number one choice for the point guard position. Josh Erickson, who was a teammate and friend, seemed to be the future guard for the Celtics.

Grayson's dad, Steve, felt that McNary never had the confidence in his son. When he was put on JV for the summer league, they did not treat him like an investment for the program. It was predetermined without seeing how much he could improve over the summer.

"I didn't think that McNary's decision was fair, and again, this was just his mother and I that felt this way – Grayson didn't feel that way. We knew that his playing style was not fitting in with the basketball program," Steve said.

George Libbon, one of Steve's customers at the jewelry store, was the men's basketball coach at Chemeketa Community College in Salem. Steve inquired about the possibility of Grayson coming out to play with the college players during the summer. He could get George's opinion of how Grayson blended with college players.

George was very accommodating and welcomed Grayson to come out and play pickup ball with his players. Steve thought that maybe Grayson could be a walk-on player there after high school – if George liked the way he played.

Grayson played pickup ball with Chemeketa's players the next opportunity he got.

"Wow! Your son can play ball. He's a great player – he's so little," George said.

When Steve heard what George said, this gave him the assurance that maybe Grayson could play at the next level and that maybe he was right about his son's talent.

Playing JV basketball his junior year was very depressing for Grayson. Probably the most depressed he had been in high school. Josh was going to be playing point guard and Grayson would be playing the two-guard position. His attitude was a little rebellious, and he started hanging out with a so called "cool crowd" that happened to be ball players. Grayson was never involved with any kind of drug experimenting, but did hang out with some kids that were of that nature.

This was also a time that he struggled a little with his parents. He felt like they were being way too strict with him. He wanted to play at Marion Square Park – streetball. At night he would play with several friends until the late hours. He was experiencing a little rebellion. I think most kids in high school experience that with their parents – part of growing up.

"Josh was a point guard that was focused on what college coaches looked for. I thought I was better. But now that I look back, Josh was a better defender and all-around player than I was at that time," Grayson said.

Steve and Molly had relatives that were involved with Salem Academy, a Christian school in Salem. This private school had a smaller enrollment and played in the Tri-River League – smaller schools. The Bouchers really liked the basketball program there and were having thoughts of transferring Grayson before his senior year.

"We thought that Salem Academy would be a great fit for Grayson. He would be at a Christian school and he would have the opportunity to play point guard there. Although the kids there were not quite like him, we still thought this would be good for him," Molly said.

They decided to do a little research on the school and also talk to the head coach about their basketball program. This was a possibility for the following year – he would finish out the current year at McNary.
McNary was a good school with an attendance of roughly 2,000 students. The school had a great basketball program and coaching staff, but it just wasn't working out for Grayson. He was going to be much happier at Salem Academy where the coaches would give him the green light on his playing style.
His parents talked to him about Salem Academy, and he was all for it. After his junior year, he signed up with the summer league to play with the Salem Academy Crusaders. It was the best thing that could have happened to the

Bouchers. Grayson was a leader on his team and running the point-guard position. They were competing and beating some of the biggest schools around in tournaments.

"When I was at McNary, the coaches made me feel like I wasn't a good player. I actually started thinking that ... until I came to Salem Academy. My parents always told me that I was better than what McNary thought. And I thought to myself, well, they're my parents, they're supposed to say that," Grayson said.

It was at the Corban College Silver Cross Tournament during the Thanksgiving vacation that Grayson was showing signs of maturity and leadership. He had the green light to play his game with his flashy style. Because of all the skills he acquired throughout the years, it all came together for him – a standout at the tourney. He was scoring points, making assists, getting rebounds, stealing the ball, etc.

To go along with his new job as the starting point guard, after the final game of the tourney, he walked to the center of the gym to accept an all-tournament award. His mom and dad were so overjoyed to see their son receive an award that was well earned and deserved.

"He did such an amazing job. To see him actually walk up and receive the All-Tournament Award along with the Tourney MVP Award was indescribable. Everything turned out great. McNary had the point guard that fit their style of play and Salem Academy didn't hold our son back from his potential. He was happier than ever playing with the Crusaders. I felt like that was the beginning of a journey," his mom said.

He was a young boy that was somewhat held back from his possibilities but became a young man full of confidence.

Head Coach Colby Molan at Salem Academy was very supportive of his new point guard. Not only did he give Grayson the green light, but he also wanted more of his playing style. The crossovers, behind-the-back passes, shooting, fast breaks, etc. It was excitement for the fans and motivating for his teammates.

Grayson had established a great relationship with his new coach. This coach even played pickup basketball on weekends with the kids.

"I love Colby as a person and coach. He was the first high school coach I ever played for that had a ton of confidence in me. He was also the first coach that utilized my strengths to benefit the team," Grayson said.

One of the highlights of Boucher's senior year was the game against East Linn Christian School. The opponents had a big post player, J.D. Hill, he was a dominate force in the league. Salem Academy managed to pull off the victory. Grayson scored 38 points to lead all scorers. The newspaper was calling him "Hurricane Boucher!"

Another highlight game was against Blanchet Catholic School. Blanchet had Anthony Godlove, a solid point guard that could shoot, handle the ball, and play defense. He was a talented kid and about the same height as Grayson. It was a great match up – the two outstanding point guards of the league.

With a sold-out crowd at Salem Academy, Grayson won the battle of the point guards. He crossed over and drove to the left on Anthony and hit fifteen-foot jumpers repeatedly. Anthony made Boucher work hard, but it was all worth it in the end. Salem Academy came out on top. I was actually at that game – I wouldn't have missed it for the world.

By the time the season started winding down, Salem Academy was sitting on a position to possibly advance to the State Tournament. After all the situations Grayson had been through and now his senior year of high school, how sweet would it be to advance to the state tournament?

In the final playoff game, they would be playing Travis Lulay and the rival Regis Rams from Stayton, Oregon – the winner would advance. Travis was a heck of an athlete – he played quarterback in football as well. Before this game, Salem Academy had a post player with talent that decided to quit the team. He wanted to focus on higher academic opportunities. He was a smart kid with a lot of potential, but for personal reasons he quit.

Grayson was a little disappointed because Regis was a tough team and they needed a strong post player to rebound and help defend Travis and company. The timing was not good and now they had to face a tough opponent that was standing in the way of a state-tournament berth.

The game was close all the way through. Grayson was fighting hard along with his teammates. But it was the final play of the game that cost them – a painful heartbreaker. A one-play mishap on the inbound during the last minute of the game … this prevented Salem Academy from advancing to state.

"It killed us. It was very disappointing – his senior year and his last chance to make it to state. We wanted that so bad for our son and the team," his dad said.

The next morning Grayson never talked about the game. It just wasn't his style to dwell on something that had already happened. His parents on the other hand were very disappointed and took it to heart. They wanted what many parents want for their kids, to make it to the state tournament and experience that exciting event.

When Grayson was selected to be one of the players representing the West in the Oregon East vs. West All-Star Game, his parents felt a lot better and more relaxed. It's a real honor to play with some of the best players in the state. Playing in a highly-respected game like the all-star game was an excellent way to cap his high school basketball career.

Shortly after the season was over, Grayson continued playing basketball at Marion Square Park in Salem, Oregon, until the midnight hour and sometimes later. He would drive out there with basketball friends. He would also play at Jake and Matt Espinoza's backyard court until midnight. The neighbors around would have to hear the ball bouncing for hours at night – serious "ballers" in the backyard. These kids had a passion for basketball. They wanted to improve their skills to the highest potential while hanging out together.

Steve Boucher had not heard anything from George Libbon, the Chemeketa C. C. coach. Chemeketa is located on the northeast side of Salem on Lancaster Drive. Some people call this community college "UCLA," University of Chemeketa on Lancaster Avenue – of course, it's a joke.

"I was starting to worry because George had not called us. I was beginning to wonder if he was interested in Grayson at all. I called George and asked if my son was going to be able to play at Chemeketa," Steve said.

"Yeah!" George responded.

The plan for Grayson was for him to be a red-shirt freshman – Libbon was a little scared of his size. Grayson was about 5' 9" at the time. He was to build up his strength and grow more to bang heads with the big kids. This would give him two more years of eligibility. George had confidence for the future. He liked the way this small kid played.

"When I started playing college basketball, I was scared of the bigger guys. In high school it was all good, but at this level they were a lot bigger. The thought of getting hit by one was nerve-racking to me," Grayson said.

This young man feared that he might not be as good as the college players. He was the last one on the team in line. He was playing with many great athletes – basically star players from their high school teams.

When the season got going, an injury to one of the point guards forced George Libbon to bring Grayson out of red-shirt status.

That timing couldn't have been better. He was going to be able to show everyone that he could compete with college players. He was playing alongside 6' 2" Greg O'Neil and 7' 0" Chris Botez – two of the best players in the league. Yes sir, he was fitting in very well. Some games he would get in for a few minutes and other games he would play fifteen minutes. He stood out pretty well for two or three games and learned a whole lot. He put himself in a position for a better second year at Chemeketa.

"The next spring, away with my fear, I started working harder than ever – I broke loose. I was playing with players that brought my confidence level up," Grayson said.

Grayson never really had any kind of issues with teammates other than competitiveness. It was one player going heads up with another for a position or making a play – during practice or during a game, it didn't matter.

In the spring after his first year at Chemeketa, something happened that would change Grayson's life and future plans. What most people don't know is that he was always watching something called "streetball." This style of play was not for everyone, but there was something about it that was electrifying.

His friends started talking about the And 1 Mixtape videos that were out on the market. You could purchase a product at Footaction or Foot Locker and receive the tape free. At that time the newest one out was the And 1 Mixtape Vol. 2 which featured Waliyy Dixon, also known as "Main Event." He was famous for his high flying dunks. A lot of these streetball athletes had earned their nicknames through their flashy style of play. Names like, Half-Man Half-Amazing, Speedy, Shane "The Dribbling Machine" Woney, AO, 50, Escalade, Hot Sauce, Headache, Sik Wit It, Prime Objective, Go Get It, The Pharmacist, and Alimoe "The Black Widow." A lot of these athletes played at the famous Rucker Park in New York, where some of best streetball players came from.

Grayson went to Foot Locker with one of his friends to buy a product and he received the tape free. Back in those days it was a VHS tape not a DVD or Blu-ray Disc. When he saw the tape, his eyes lit up – a passion dwelled in his heart. He fell in love with the style of play and wanted to learn as many moves as he could. Later on, he had to go back and pick up the And 1 Mixtape Vol. 1 which is the tape that started it all.

Grayson was watching this tape with Matt and Jake Espinoza, some good friends and teammates from McNary High School. It was such a fascination, how these guys handled the ball bouncing it off of a player's head and crossing over the defender. The amazing dunks and dimes (assists) were worth the time to sit and watch – very exciting stuff. In streetball, there's no such thing as "carrying the ball" or "traveling." That's probably one of the reasons some coaches don't like kids viewing this style of play. But this was a form of entertainment and still is today as I see it.

It was the And 1 Mixtape Vol. 1 that started this whole adventure. Rafer Alston, also known as "Skip to My Lou," was the defining player that made And 1 what it became. He was the main focus of Vol 1. His dazzling moves and his flashy dribbling, passing, and shooting, were a sight to catch. In fact, his nickname stands for one of his moves. He was the first streetball player to sign an endorsement deal with And 1.

"When I saw Rafer's moves and incredible talent, I knew this was something I was meant for and definitely wanted to be a part of. Rafer inspired me to work on moves and even for me to try my own inventions," Grayson said.

Keep in mind that Grayson was a sophomore in high school when all of this fascination with streetball began. The And 1 players would tour around the country, playing to entertain crowds at high school gyms. Grayson got word that they were coming to Jefferson High School in Portland. He decided to drive up with his brother, Landon. They were filming the open runs (games that local players were involved in as well).

When the next And 1 Mixtape Volume was out – Grayson saw that he made it for a small clip. It wasn't much, but he was in it. This tape made him want to improve more. He took it to the next level – started dribbling between player's legs and bouncing it off their heads. He would play at Marion Square Park and applied what he learned. He would amaze anyone watching.

In the spring of 2003, after his first year of college at Chemeketa, Grayson was working at a local grocery store. He got word that the And 1 Mixtape Tour was touring many cities including Portland. This was the second season presented by the And 1 shoe company. The new season was being sponsored by Mountain Dew Code Red. This new ESPN TV show *Streetball* was aired weekly. The tour's goal was to have an open run, select two or three players to play in the evening game, and then select a talented individual to join the tour. NBA players (from time to time) and other streetball legends would play with the locals against the And 1 Team inside NBA arenas. After the game the And 1 Team would vote for one local person to join them on the tour. They would then eliminate one person that didn't make the cut from a previous city. Some people might call it the American Idol of basketball. And 1 would offer a contract (including a paid salary) to the newest legend chosen at the end of the season tour. This player would have to outlast every player selected throughout the cities toured.

The tour started in Tacoma, Washington, and the second stop was Portland, Oregon. The tour would continue with Sacramento, California; Oakland, California; Los Angeles, California; Phoenix, Arizona; Dallas, Texas; Houston, Texas; Jackson, Mississippi; New Orleans, Louisiana; Birmingham, Alabama; Detroit, Michigan; New York City, New York; Toronto, Canada; Indianapolis, Indiana; Cleveland, Ohio; Columbus, Ohio; Chicago, Illinois; Louisville, Kentucky; Kansas City, Missouri; Miami, Florida; Tampa, Florida; Raleigh, North Carolina; Atlanta, Georgia; Baltimore, Maryland; Washington DC; Lowell, Massachusetts; Trenton, New Jersey; New York City, New York (Madison Square Garden); Philadelphia, Pennsylvania; and finally end at Linden, New Jersey.

An open run was held at the Portland stop. Once again Grayson drove up to Portland with his brother, Landon. The location this time was at the Rose Quarters, where they were holding the open run outdoors. Several players (if selected) would earn the opportunity to play against the And 1 Team in the evening game, which would be a paid admission game. This would be an opportunity for the locals to showcase their streetball talent for a chance to ride on the bus and be part of the And 1 Mixtape Tour. They would try to remain on the tour until being voted off.

"We knew about him and Landon driving up to Portland for the open run. We were at Detroit Lake when that happened. Molly and I really thought that it was just some pickup game in Portland," Steve said.

It was a sunny day and the weather could not have been better. During the open run Grayson tore it up. He was showcasing his talent. Dribbling through the defender's legs and getting close enough to move the basketball around the defender's neck and grabbing the basketball again before throwing a dime (an assist) or scoring an easy lay-up. The crowd was roaring with excitement. I remember watching him on the TV local news.

Waliyy Dixon, also known as "Main Event" was one of the spokesmen for *Streetball*, the ESPN TV Show. He explained that they were looking for the next streetball legend. Each member of the And 1 Team would vote on their choice, but it was Main Event that had the final say.

Grayson was one of three players picked to play in the evening game – an experience that will never be forgotten. This clean-cut kid from Keizer, Oregon, would get his chance at something beyond imaginable.

"I'm excited to play with Hot Sauce, Alimoe and all those guys. I've seen them on TV – this is like a dream. You know what I mean?" Grayson looked into the camera.

Skip to My Lou had moved on to the NBA, but would make appearances to play against the And 1 Team from time to time. Grayson played against, Philip Champion, also known as "Hot Sauce," one of the most popular players on the And 1 team. Hot Sauce was definitely a talented streetball player that could shut the gym down with some of his moves – breaking ankles (when a defender falls due to a sudden change of direction from the offensive player) along with ball handles that impressed many viewers. Sometimes, Hot Sauce would reach over and grab the back part of the defender's shirt, and pull it over the face blinding him. Hot Sauce did this while dribbling, then he would drive for the score. The crowd would go wild! He was definitely a showboat.

During the game Grayson was a highlight with all of his own ridiculous moves and sharp shooting. The competition was tough with Big Mike (who traveled with the team) coaching the locals against the And 1 Team. Master of Ceremonies was none other than Duke Tango – the And 1 voice during the game. We'll talk more about him a little later.

At the end of the night it was time for a vote from the And 1 team. It came down to the final two. Grayson Boucher and Jalonte Martin were the two players being discussed. For these two players it was a nerve-racking situation to be in after a long night of hard work.

The And 1 Team selected both of them to go on tour starting at Phoenix. There was a sigh of relief from Grayson and Jalonte. They were both to continue touring with the And 1 Mixtape Tour. But first they would prepare to say goodbye to their families and friends.

"When we got the news we were very happy for Grayson. But at the same time I was worried. He was only nineteen and I was going to miss him dearly," Molly said.

For parents to receive great news like that about their son is an unbelievable feeling. A start of a new adventure that was unexpected. Grayson was being interviewed by the local media.

"I'm speechless, it feels good. I actually came out here and did something," Grayson said.

Grayson didn't give it a second thought. He felt in his heart that he belonged there. Of course it was very difficult to be leaving his family – he was so close to them. His brother Landon was always his biggest fan, he was never envious. Landon was so excited for his brother to have an opportunity like that. The two brothers went everywhere together for years. A bitter-sweet situation, Landon was Grayson's best friend.

"As a parent I would have loved for Grayson to have continued college basketball and complete his education. But I had never seen him this happy before. I knew that's what he wanted to do. This was an opportunity that not many kids get. He can always go back to school later in life when he gets the time," Steve said.

Boucher was about to live his dream playing on the And 1 Mixtape Tour. He had no idea how long he would last before possibly getting voted off, but he was going to live that moment to the fullest.
Grayson was given a week to pack and to say his goodbyes. During that time the tour continued with stops at Sacramento, Oakland, and Los Angeles – more competition for the young blonde kid to deal with.
When the week flew by, he would head out to Portland International Airport to catch his flight. Jalonte did not show up and missed his flight. So it was just Grayson joining the

team for the next big-city stop. This 2003 And 1 Mixtape Tour earned the opportunity to play their games in NBA arenas. The ESPN TV Show had grown that much and by this time there were six And 1 Mixtape Volumes on the market.

The first stop away from home was Phoenix, Arizona. Grayson had to bring his "A" game every day during the tour. He was putting out his best effort to avoid getting eliminated from the tour. And it seemed like every city would have an amazing player he had to compete against to survive the cut.

When arriving at Phoenix, Grayson had no clue what was about to happen. You could see Headache's big smile as he called Grayson. The And 1 players would make him carry their luggage. Alimoe, also known as "Black Widow" made him run sprints on the parking lot. There were other selected activities as well – a form of hazing in a humorous way. At one point they even made him carry a doll everywhere he went. Are you kidding me? A large doll! That had to be embarrassing – but that was the point.

"I'll do whatever it takes to stay on this tour," Grayson said.

Troy Jackson, also known as "Escalade," who is the brother of Mark Jackson (former NBA player and current coach of the Golden State Warriors), took a liking to Grayson. He became his mentor and started showing him the ropes of the And 1 team. When you see these two together they're definitely not twins. Escalade was a Black man, 6' 10" 400 lbs. Grayson was a White skinny kid at 5' 10" and maybe 150 lbs. at the time.

"They just fell in love with Grayson and embraced him as part of their family. No one would have guessed what was happening – naturally we were very proud of our son," Steve said.

Skip to My Lou had just played against the And 1 Team at the Los Angeles stop – just before the Phoenix stop. Grayson missed the opportunity to play against the player that inspired him to be part of this adventure. At Los Angeles they had also picked up a Black kid at 5' 8" with amazing hops. He could dunk the ball ridiculously! Dennis Chism, also known as "Spyda," could light up the stadium because of his leaping ability. The kid would be Grayson's competition the entire tour.

Boucher's nickname was given to him by the emcee of the And 1 Mixtape Tour, Duke Tango, a short chunky older Black man that wore a crazy hat at each game. Duke had a voice that would bring excitement to the streetball games. He would actually go out to the floor and engage with the crowd and players while the game was in progress. Duke would yell at the top of his lungs about amazing passes or who got schooled. That's where he got the nickname idea for the skinny White kid from Oregon.

This kid was dribbling the lights out of the ball and taking the defenders to school – breaking ankles and throwing dimes around them. Grayson was educating the defenders according to Duke.

"The Professor! ... The Professor! ... My Godson! ... Here he comes!" Duke Tango would yell on the microphone as Grayson dribbled down court.

Duke Tango was known for giving new breed the nicknames. He had the ability to watch the talent and come up with a name that fit. The nickname "The Professor" was like the fire chasing the gasoline on a rope across the nation overnight. I call it an overnight sensation. He was the only

White kid on the team and one of the youngest by far – definitely an age gap. Everyone was talking about The Professor.

At Phoenix he was remarkable – he now had his own nickname. After the game was over, Shane "The Dribbling Machine" Woney walked up to The Professor.

"Good work! You might stay another week," Shane said.

The And 1 crew was excited about having Boucher on tour, the newest streetball player with a legit shot at becoming a legend. No one would have thought this kid from Oregon would be a legend his first year on tour, but if you watched him play you would think otherwise.

A lot of the attention was focused on Philip Champion, also known as "Hot Sauce," until The Professor came on board. At the Dallas stop it was all about Hot Sauce. Duke Tango started calling him "Hot Sizzle" a few times. Grayson had ball handles to match Hot Sauce's.

At the Houston stop, Compaq Center, a defining moment was about to happen. Toward the end of the game with a huge crowd on hand, there were seconds left. The And 1 Team was ahead 77-76. The Professor, Spyda, Roberto (picked up in Sacramento) along with other talent were trailing and about to inbound the ball. As the clock was about to expire, with the crowd on their feet, the ball came to The Professor. He turned and let it go flipping his wrist. What a nice moment, he knocked it down – a huge three-point shot to win the game! The crowd went mad and a great portion of them instantly became Professor fans. The kid from Salem/Keizer shut the gym down.

After the game, Grayson had to do twenty pushups for embarrassing the And 1 Team. It was all good and it gave him valuable air-time minutes on *Streetball*.

During that stop in Houston, Roberto, who was Grayson's roommate for the tour, injured his ankle severely. He was Grayson's friend and closer to his age – he could relate more to him than the older guys on the team. Unfortunately, he was voted off due to the injury – a very sad day for Roberto whose wife was expecting a child back home.

"I was really hoping to make it. Now I gotta go back home and take care of my responsibilities – get a job ... take care of my family. Watch out for The Professor, kid got game ... mad game," Roberto said as he exited.

By the time the tour arrived in New Orleans, The Professor was becoming a huge part of And 1. Throughout the season as the tour bus arrived at a new city, you could see the large crowds waiting for the team. They seemed to form a long line on both sides of the street.

"Professor! Professor!" Many people would yell with their hands up waving.

The players would roll down the bus windows and wave at the crowd. Before games and after games, The Professor would sign autographs along with the And 1 Team. This was only if time allowed.

His dad, Steve, caught the next flight to New Orleans, Louisiana, where the next game would take place. He was about to see his son play live for the first time since he left on tour. But not only that, it was his son ... and he missed him. Grayson had the same feelings. To see family again was a delightful joy.

Duke Tango gave Steve a nickname, "The Jeweler," a perfect name for Steve. He was also interviewed and received airtime on the ESPN TV Show. Some of footage was taken down Bourbon Street. For some of you that might not know about Bourbon Street in New Orleans, well, just put it this way, you won't get any sleep there.

"I'd like to say that he gets his talent from me, but ...," Steve said in front of the camera, "It's really neat to see him play in a big arena."

Grayson was starting to get used to being called Professor wherever he went. It was a different world for him and he didn't really know how to respond to people. He was just being himself and he absorbed all of the attention he was getting from fans, the media, etc.

"It started feeling a little strange to me at one point. When I was at malls people started following me around everywhere I went. If I sat down to eat, people would just come up to me and sit at my table – I didn't even know them. People were hitting me up all the time. I didn't get it. I was new and had never experienced any of this. I learned quickly how to embrace fans," Grayson said.

At each city, after the games, there were autograph lines formed around the players. The Professor watched reactions from all sorts of fans. Some women would cry when they got to meet him. People act different when they see a celebrity up close. Everyone wanted their picture taken with the Professor.

"Now, anywhere I go, I just expect craziness. I've gotten used to it," Grayson said.

Grayson loved to play basketball anywhere. The challenges he would face as his popularity arouse was mostly by players at gyms or outdoor parks. It seemed like there was always someone challenging him – trying to prove they were better. He couldn't just have fun playing basketball.

"Players that saw me on ESPN knew me and I automatically became a target for them to want to be better than me – always some kind of competition or challenge," he said.

Yes sir, The Professor was heating up and people were starting to wonder if he might be better than Hot Sauce. Of course this made a great conflict for the TV show.

I remember watching a sports show where they were interviewing Rafer Alston, also known as "Skip to My Lou." The question was asked to Skip. Who do you think has the best ball handles right now?

"As surprisingly as it might sound, I personally think The Professor," Rafer said.

Wow! Rafer Alston said this – the Streetball legend that defined And 1. That was such a huge compliment to Grayson. And we're talking about his competition being Rafer himself, Hot Sauce, Sik Wit It, Shane, and more legends. Rafer then backed up his comment by saying he was a little rusty on streetball handles due to the NBA skill set and followed it with a smile.

The tour finally arrived at Detroit, Michigan. With fans going crazy as they saw the And 1 tour buses come into the city, you could see the players waving at them. Detroit was one of Grayson's biggest moments during the tour.

Inside Cobo Center in front of a large crowd, The Professor was defending Hot Sauce. Hot Sauce crossed him over. Professor slipped a little and Hot Sauce had an open three-point shot. He took the shot and knocked it down – the crowd was roaring!

"When anyone plays in a streetball game, you just don't want to be in the position I was in ... trust me," Grayson said.

The next time around The Professor had the ball and Hot Sauce was defending him. It's really difficult to describe the move he put on Hot Sauce, but you could see the fire in Grayson's eyes – hungry for revenge. He was using his right hand sending the ball between his legs from the left side. Then he glided sideways like Michael Jackson while dribbling the ball. Hot Sauce was caught in confusion. Professor then crossed him over and drove left for the easy score. That shut Cobo Center down, he received a louder applause! Everyone was on their feet, stomping and yelling. Some fans were even rolling on the ground!

"I had thoughts of going back to school, but that moment let me know that this is where I belong," Grayson said.

The tour continued and The Professor fan base was growing by the minute. There were signs being held up by many. One girl had a sign that read, "Professor Will You Marry Me?" Another read, "We Love U Professor."
Some of the And 1 Players started feeling a little envy toward Grayson because of all the attention he was getting. Some of the players felt that he hadn't really earned his nickname and that the legends were being disrespected.
All of the jealous adventure slowly wore itself out and the players were beginning to accept the fact that The Professor was earning his stay with his talents.

"It was kind of hard to take in at the time. I think being 19 years old I didn't understand why they would be upset. I was more hurt at that time. But as time went by the guys started showing more support of me being on the team and contributing," Grayson said.

When the tour came to Toronto, Canada, Grayson would finally play with Skip to My Lou, the streetball legend who inspired him. After the game he shook his hand and exchanged a few words. That was a nice moment for Grayson and well deserved.

When the shows were aired they basically took the highlights of the most exciting plays during the game and pieced them together. With Grayson being a White kid that could play the game with his flashy style, well, that was definitely a piece that And 1 really needed. The fans were really embracing the entire concept including me (one of his biggest fans). What a nice addition to the tour.

Sometimes there were online surveys that fans could take to vote. They could pick the player they felt should stay on the tour. According to Troy Jackson, also known as "Escalade," 85 percent of the votes would be for The Professor. That's a pretty big fan base. Unfortunately that didn't matter, because it was up to the And 1 Team with the final vote going to Main Event.

After the Chicago stop there was some support from Escalade on The Professor's behalf. The longer The Professor remained on the tour, the more supportive Escalade was beginning to be.

"He's a very good kid and a very good player," Escalade said.

Dennis Chism, also known as "Spyda" was interviewed as well. This talented athlete knew he was up against a kid that had a lot going for him.

"We all know everybody wants Professor to win," Spyda said.

Spyda didn't really need to prove anything to anyone – his dazzling dunks and spectacular drives to the bucket were mind boggling. When I met him at one of the games I actually doubted he was only 5' 8" but surely enough, I'd say either 5' 7" or 5' 8". What Spyda didn't have, was the mad-ball handles that The Professor had.

The discussions on the bus continued with some of the And 1 players having a difficult time accepting the newest talent discovered in Portland, Oregon. They saw The Professor as a threat maybe, or just jealousy, who knows.

There were times where Hot Sauce would grab The Professor just so he wouldn't dribble around him for the easy bucket. That caused problems with Duke Tango. During some of the bus rides Duke would get into a yelling bout – mostly directed at Hot Sauce for holding The Professor intentionally during the game.

"I bet Professor beats you one-on-one if you don't hold him every time he drives on you!" Duke yelled.

By the time the squad reached Miami, Florida, several new players that had made a run for it were voted off – Night Train and Hard Work. In Miami, NBA player, Ricky Davis was a guest player. One of the nice things about Grayson being part of the tour was meeting all sorts of high profile athletes. In Tampa, Florida, Shaquille O'Neal (NBA Player) and Warren Sapp (NFL Player) were in the building watching. They loved the streetball entertainment.

In Atlanta, Georgia, NBA players, Dikembe Mutombo, Larry Hughes, and Ricky Davis were in the building watching. Ricky Davis actually participated in the game against the And 1 Team. This was the hometown of Spyda and Hot Sauce – exciting evening for the two.

New names started coming up as the cities went by, and Grayson was still surviving the cut night after night. Hometown Kid, Helicopter, Magic, and J-Dubb were more streetball players discovered with amazing talent.

"When you see this kid called The Helicopter ... oooh Baby!" Duke Tango said.

Duke was correct. John Humphrey, also known as "Helicopter," was a Black kid, 6' 0" tall and could leap out of the gym. All of these players had muscular physiques – they stayed in great shape. This gave The Professor an opportunity to showcase some passes to Helicopter. Professor would come down dribbling and get up in the air passing the ball between his legs toward Helicopter. Helicopter would then slam dunk it as he caught it above the rim – such excitement that brought the house down!

At New York, Madison Square Garden, something happened that made me feel Grayson had earned his celebrity status, nickname, respect, or whatever else you might want to call it.

The And 1 Team was up 70-69 with seconds left. It was a jam-packed Madison Square Garden – a near sold-out crowd. Big Mike was coaching the locals with other legends. I think everyone knew that The Professor was going to get the ball. They were correct, Professor ran up to the top left a few feet behind NBA range. That was the only place they were going to let him have the ball. As soon as he caught the rock from the inbound pass, he turned around and shot it with time running out ... it sailed awhile in the air – swoosh! Game over. The crowd was going crazy! – unbelievable. His entire team came after him and mobbed him for the victory celebration. The serious confidence in The Professor's face said it all.

"I just let it go! I knew it was going in right when I let it go," he smiles.

This was the one place Grayson had dreamed of playing a basketball game. A lot of history in that arena and a big-time basketball spot – the Mecca. Not only does he get to play there but he wins a game with a clutch shot with no time left. How cool is that?

In the locker room the And 1 players were disappointed that they lost the game. It was quiet ... when they looked at Escalade for an answer – they had to accept the fact that this kid deserved to be where he was at.

"Professor just hit a game-winning shot in front of 10,000 people," Escalade said.

The tour came to an end at the final stop. Linden, New Jersey, home of Waliyy Dixon, also known as "Main Event." The next day following the evening game, the team still wanted to see The Professor, Helicopter, and Spyda play outdoors at the park. They wanted to see the finalist play real streetball at the park mixed with the And 1 players. They would then make a final decision of who would win the contract. It came down to those three in the end. At the outdoor park, Professor was sensational, especially seeing him go at Hot Sauce and winning the battle.

After that game they got around in a circle and each player voted on their choice. It was nerve-racking seeing the players announce their picks. Not everyone voted for The Professor, but not everyone voted for Spyda or Helicopter either. The votes were tallied in front of everyone.

"And this year's contract winner and newest streetball legend is ... El Professor," said Antony Hayward, also known as "Half-Man Half-Amazing."

Grayson received his And 1 Team jersey that had his nickname on the back and a big number 12 on it.

"Forget bagging groceries," Grayson walks away with his jersey and teammates.

Grayson signed a contract with And 1 and traveled with the team the following year and several after that. He learned many valuable lessons during this experience. Some were very difficult. Escalade became like a big brother to him. The age gap was such a difference that he found himself staying at hotels with the few players that didn't party like some of the others did. It just wasn't his thing.

They toured 18 cities in Europe and the fans were amazing. Spyda and Helicopter had joined the And 1 Team by then. They had huge crowds showing up at every game. Signing autographs, photo shoots, commercials, etc. was routine. Being away from home took a toll, but being away from his country was a nightmare.

"The Europe tour was the time that I was probably the unhappiest. I couldn't connect with anyone – I didn't know the languages. Most of the guys would want to chase after chicks and party. I wasn't into that," Grayson said.

Grayson wandered away from the hotel one evening. He was going to make a phone call to talk to some family. How difficult can it be to find your way back to the hotel? He was thinking this in his mind. Well, he got lost and could not find his way back. He asked a few people, but he could not understand a word they were saying. His mouth started feeling dry and his palms sweaty – he was almost to the point of actually crying. He continued walking and looking everywhere. After a few blocks he finally saw his hotel and felt a huge relief.

He fought through those hard times. Spyda was his roommate and closer to his age while Escalade was like a big brother and mentor to him. That made it possible for him not to feel too depressed. He could actually hang out and do things with them.

In 2004, Grayson traveled to Australia with two of his teammates – John Harvey, also known as "High Octane" and Robert Martin, also known as "50." They signed a deal to play in the Australian National 3-On-3 Tournament. According to Grayson, this was one of his most exciting and memorable moments. The large crowds embraced the And 1 players. They played in many exhibitions before playing in the championship game against the best Australian team. And 1 won the game.

In 2005, playing in Brazil in front of 19,000 people – a sold-out crowd, was amazing for The Professor. The request for another game was so high in demand there, that they scheduled another game on the following Monday. That game drew 17,000 people.

In Tokyo Japan, best game ever for The Professor in front of another sold-out crowd. Streetball was huge in Japan, and they all knew The Professor.

"I remember when I first watched myself on TV with my friends. I was nervous. I didn't like hearing myself talk. I guess I didn't like a lot of attention. But when I was in front of a large crowd like those games in Brazil and Japan, well, I can't describe the great feeling. It was amazing to have had the opportunity to play there," Grayson said.

In Los Angeles, California, at a game, The Professor was about to receive some amazing news. Director Brin Hill was looking for an actor to cast in a movie *Ball Don't Lie*. This movie was based on a novel "Ball Don't Lie" by Matt de la Pena. Brin was sitting on a front-row seat at the game. As Grayson was leaving the floor Brin handed him the script. He knew it was the only way he could get the script to The Professor. Brin knew it would be very difficult to go through all the red tape – this was much easier. He was very interested in Grayson joining the cast. He asked Grayson to read the script and get back to him if he was interested in playing that part.

They needed a White kid that could play basketball with a flashy style. Grayson would be perfect for the role of Sticky, a child that was passed from foster home to foster home. And even better, he would play a lead role in a movie.

"I didn't know what to say, I had never done acting – not even in high school. But I really wanted to have this opportunity," Grayson said.

He immediately read the script and was excited to be part of this movie. He contacted Brin right away. In 2006, he enrolled in acting lessons immediately. He endured a crash course in four months to be prepared as much as he could. Four months is not enough time to become a great actor, but for the type of movie he would be shooting, it served as enough time.

"I loved it! I never thought I'd ever do something like that. I feared public speaking for a long time. But when I did this, I overcame all that fear and enjoyed every minute of it," Grayson said.

Some of the main actors in this movie would be Kim Hidalgo (played the role of Sticky's girlfriend), Rosanna Arquette, Chris "Ludacris" Bridges, Nick Cannon, and Dania Ramirez would also be in the film. This was an exciting time for Grayson and his family.

"Yes, it was very exciting at first. We knew about him taking acting lessons and the movie for so long, but then it just dragged for such a long time that we didn't know if it was ever going to be released," Steve Boucher said.

In 2008, the movie *Ball Don't Lie* was finally released to some film festivals across the country. The ones I knew of were the Tribeca Film Festival and the Seattle Film Festival. My wife Loni and I traveled to Seattle, which is about four hours from Salem, Oregon. One of my sons was coaching that day and the other was performing in a concert at the time. My boys and I were close friends with Grayson and they really wanted to come but couldn't. It was there at the Seattle Film Festival that we watched the film. We had the honor of hanging out with Grayson after the show. It was really cool, because Grayson and Kim were both there to answer questions after the film. What was my opinion of the movie? I thought they used Grayson very well in the film, he did an amazing job. He was definitely the star of the movie. If you like basketball, action, romance, and conflicts, you would love this movie. This movie could actually happen in real life. We were all very proud of Grayson.

"It was crazy! While I was on tour, I'd fly back during the week to shoot the film and then the weekend would come up and I'd fly back to join the tour. It was tiring but well worth the effort," Grayson said.

It was beginning to be a very busy life ... and when he got the chance he would visit his family and friends back in Oregon. He made Los Angeles his home. He liked the weather and all the many things to do there.

Boucher also played an extra in the movie *Semi-Pro*, with Woody Harrelson and Will Ferrell. While at a pre-basketball camp for the actors, before shooting on the set, Woody kept mentioning to Grayson that he should play him a game. Grayson finally decided to go for it. The actors were in a circle watching this. The Professor and Woody (from the old TV series *Cheers*) were set to play one-on-one. Woody gets the ball first.

"I didn't think I should start out too strong so I let him have a few shots. He actually made a few shots on me right away. So he had one or two baskets on me. I started playing defense on him. I got the ball, and after that, it was over. I killed him 30 – 4," Grayson said.

To see that action off set would have been a great moment. I can imagine the talk around there when Woody had a four-point lead. But then The Professor took over and didn't turn back. According to Grayson, Woody was a good sport and was laughing a lot of the time.

Once again The Professor would bounce on another plane and head to another tour. It was beginning to be his life – very busy. Often in foreign countries Grayson would experience surprising things. In America the situation would be entirely different.

In Puerto Rico, Grayson and Troy Jackson, also known as "Escalade," went out walking in the city. They had a meal and afterward started walking back to the hotel. They noticed two policemen following them about fifty yards behind.

"We started worrying about what we might have done wrong. We didn't want to get into any trouble. We kept walking back to the hotel and finally made it to our room," Grayson said.

While in their hotel room, they received a phone call asking them to please come down to the lobby. The fear of not knowing the reason for the call was quite alarming. As they walked down the hallway they could see that it was the same two policemen waiting for them.

"Basically, they were fans of ours and just wanted to get our autographs," Grayson said laughing, "Escalade would have told this story a lot better than me."

While touring overseas, Grayson encountered one of the scariest moments of his life. In 2010 in Angola, Africa, while doing an outdoor basketball clinic, The Professor would face a near-death experience.

"Angola, Africa was an awesome time, and the people there were amazing. They were really into streetball. I remember at the basketball clinic it was super hot and humid," Grayson said.

That evening he could not sleep, he was sweating, kept waking up and felt really ill. Linda, who was traveling with the team, asked if he needed to go to the doctor. At first he wasn't sure, but then he started feeling feverish, dizzy, and weak. Things got worse and Linda took him to the doctor.

In a third-world country the technology in medicine is not as advanced compared to the United States. Grayson needed medical attention. The doctor did not talk English but was alarmed by what she saw.

"What's wrong, what is it?" Grayson asked.

The doctor's jaw dropped and her eyes opened wide. Grayson had mosquito bites everywhere. The doctor said he had Malaria, a mosquito-born infectious disease that could result in a coma or death. After some tests and confirming, they immediately put him in quarantine (isolated from anyone else) since it was contagious. Grayson was scared and had no choice but to remain in Angola, Africa, for treatment. The rest of the team continued the tour.

"I was freaking out! I was all alone there. I mean, the way they draw blood for tests there? It's not like in the United States. They actually pressed my arm to get the blood into these needles hooked to a tube. I couldn't eat anything for 24 hours while they administered the medicine through an IV," Grayson said.

The nurses and doctors there kept reassuring him that he was going to be okay. That helped Grayson have a more positive outlook on things. After a week of recovering he started feeling better ... including eating well again – he was starved at that point. He spent two weeks in Angola before returning home.

Malaria is a serious infectious disease. Parasites hit the liver and reproduce there and also live in the bloodstream. If not treated the person could die. Once Grayson received treatment and recovered, he could not donate blood for three years. He wouldn't be contagious unless blood came into contact with someone. After three years he would be good again – fully recovered. If he chose to, he could donate blood as well.

There were many positive things (not just negative) that came out of his touring experience with And 1. He became a better speaker due to all of the interviews and public appearances he was making. He learned how to communicate better with different cultures. He was better educated in the business world – business deals, contracts etc. Knowing all of the legal technicalities, he felt like he had a college education already. Boucher also became more of a leader for his team as well.

Touring with And 1 was an experience that will never be forgotten for Grayson. But with all of the good there were also some "not so good" learning experiences. Grayson was living a very expensive lifestyle. Dining, buying expensive technology toys, cars, etc. But then again, I don't know how many of us would not do the same as a 19 or 20 year-old kid.

"One of the things I learned while on tour and being in the spotlight was how to manage my money better. I actually blew about $500,000 on just buying things and living expensively, including a location close to Venice Beach. I manage my finances a lot better now," Grayson said.

And 1 Tour Coordinator from 2010 to current, Linda Hill, was good to Grayson. He was the newest streetball legend "The Professor" and he toured many countries. He was featured in six seasons of the ESPN TV Show, *Streetball*. Further, he was featured in several magazine covers such as *Sports Illustrated*, *Sole*, *Dime*, online magazine *WOHM (WeOutHere Magazine)*, and *Carter*. He was also featured in five And 1 Mixtape DVDs, four And 1 commercials, and one video game.

Sadly to say, the And 1 ESPN TV Show, *Streetball*, came to an end. The contract was not renewed due to And 1 being bought out by another company. And 1 was huge, especially in other countries. There was a lot of popularity.

All the details are not known of what really happened, but it was evident that fans still wanted to see the tour continue.

"It was such an amazing adventure. I toured through 40 countries. I feel really blessed. To see less fortunate people come up with a way to pay for the ticket to watch us play, that says a lot of how big it was," Grayson said.

In 2008, Grayson got to know Demetrious Spencer, CEO of Ball Up Streetball. This company was based in Los Angeles. And 1 was more of behind the scenes footage, Ball Up Streetball was more about on-the-court action. Grayson really liked that about Ball Up. The Professor left And 1 in 2011 due to no contract offered to any players. He signed to play with Ball Up Streetball along with several of the former And 1 Players.

The new team roster was, The Professor, Air Up There, Bone Collector, AO, Sik Wit It, Escalade, Springs, Violator, Special FX, Mr. Afrika, and Pat the Rock.

In 2012, Ball Up Streetball signed a deal with Fox Sports to air ten TV episodes beginning with a Celebrity All-Star Game. And a new adventure began for The Professor.

"With Ball Up Streetball, I'm having more fun. It's a growing brand and sounds very promising. Demetrious has big plans for the future and wants this company to be even bigger than And 1. This process is still in the works," Grayson said.

The teammates he plays with now are more of his age and better to communicate with. The Professor played in several games, but had to sit out for a few months due to an injury he sustained on his foot. He was recovering for a long time. This injury was more serious than any he had before.

Rumors started flying about The Professor. Some people thought he wasn't playing anymore. Others had their own ideas, but really he was just injured and could not go until he was well. A lot of people that came to watch The Professor were disappointed when they saw he wasn't playing.

While he was recovering, it was a great time for my son Matt and I to come visit him at his nice gated-apartment complex in Los Angeles. This gave me the time to interview him. He had some time off to rest his foot. He was starting to walk on it slowly and felt like taking a walk with us down Rodeo Drive.

We hopped into his BMW and drove to the gas station to fill up with gas. After the car was filled up with gas, we were getting ready to drive off. It didn't take long for a fan to recognize him. The gas station attendant looked at me, I was in the backseat and my son was in the passenger side.

"Excuse me sir! Is your driver The Professor?"
"Yes he is," I responded.

Grayson turns and looks at him and waves.
"Hey Professor, I like your game man!"
"Thanks," Grayson said as we drove off.

While walking and looking at sneakers in the mall, another person stopped us and wanted to know if that was The Professor.

"Hey aren't you The Professor?"
"Yeah ... how you doing?"
"I like your moves man," the shopper said.
"Thanks man," Grayson responded.

Grayson Boucher "The Professor" Earned His Streetball Name

The Professor was well known. That evening we went to eat dinner at a restaurant where we saw Motown-Legend Smokey Robinson. The owners told me that he usually orders out every Friday night. That was cool to see a music legend live and to eat dinner with a streetball legend in one night.

One of the final things we did was attend worship at Shepard Church in LA. We listened to Pastor Dudley Rutherford. Grayson has plans of spreading the Gospel through basketball. He has thoughts of doing outreach basketball clinics.

"I'd like to get Ball Up Streetball better known – it's growing super fast. I want to do some more acting, and I would also love to use basketball as a ministry tool for Gospel outreach – you know ... sports ministry type thing? I love it here in LA but I do miss my family and friends back in Oregon," Grayson said.

The parents, Steve and Molly Boucher, have done an amazing job raising this young man. I asked them what kind of advice they could give other parents.

"Let your kids follow their dreams. They're not always going to happen, but just keep them going. Tell your kids that everything is important – like a competition. You always have the result if you put in the work. Set an example for your kids. Show them that every practice is important," Steve said as Molly agreed.

Grayson "The Professor" Boucher has set a mark and continues to be successful in his passions of life. He has become a great role model for kids to learn from.

What he has accomplished despite his height and challenges is beyond imaginable. He put in the hard work that paid off and he never said he couldn't do it. He just went for it. He has recovered from his foot injury and continues to tour with Ball Up Streetball wearing his number 12 jersey with "Professor" on the back of it.

He has big plans for the future after his playing days are over. Basketball clinics with his brother Landon, acting, Gospel Outreach, and whatever else he comes up with. Look out for The Professor!

Janelle Weiss, a Determined Athlete

Janelle Weiss is thankful to Patsy T. Mink, the congresswoman that introduced Title IX back in 1972. Janelle didn't know who this lady was when I asked her. Once I filled her in on some history, she responded with excellent words.

"She made it possible for young women athletes to participate in school sports. She stood up for what she believed in. Patsy has set a mark to bless many people," Janelle said.

In my opinion, it's important for young people to know what was done years ago to make their success possible. It's impressive to see the progress that young-female athletes have made through the years. I would like to share a story about a 5' 5" point guard who signed a letter of intent to play college basketball with the University of Idaho Vandals.

Janelle Weiss was born in Salem, Oregon, in 1992. She comes from a middle-income-class family. Her parents, Paul and Earleen, have always had jobs. Her dad is an Environmental Engineer for the City of Salem and her mom is a Private Piano Lessons Instructor.

At an early age, Janelle would watch her brothers, Eric and Steven, play basketball on the street in front of their small home. The neighborhood was calm and surrounded with friends – no real trouble at all.

One day Janelle got tired of watching and decided to pick up a basketball. She started dribbling the ball and discovered she enjoyed it. After her dribbling improved, she then started shooting the basketball. Every day was an improvement as she repetitively shot the basketball.

The neighborhood was dominated by boys. Janelle started playing basketball with the boys. She wasn't very tall, but that didn't stop her. This was motivation to improve her game.

Earleen wanted her little girl to not be afraid of being a lady. Why couldn't she wear dresses now and then? Instead, she would wear her blonde shiny hair in a ponytail. She'd wear basketball shorts everywhere she went – I guess just like a tomboy. But that's who Janelle was as a young girl – very active. She wanted to play outside – she was focused and determined.

Earleen introduced her daughter to music. Playing the piano was something she would have loved Janelle to be engaged in. She encouraged Janelle to play musical instruments. Her mom wanted her to try other things and not just play basketball all the time.

"I wanted my kids to do something musical – sing or play a musical instrument. I felt that eventually they would know if that was an interest to them. If not, then at least I had introduced music to them and it was their choice to do as they wished," Earleen said.

Janelle began playing the piano and did remarkably well. One evening during a piano recital she had a bad experience – she hit bottom. There was no comfort playing the piano in front of a large crowd. In addition, she had sheet music that was not familiar to her. Things did not go well and Janelle was done with the piano adventure – that's not what she wanted to do.

"In the second grade she convinced us to let her play basketball," her mom said.

Paul and Earleen have always wanted their kids to pursue what was in their heart – to let them discover the path they wanted to choose. And with Janelle, it was evident that basketball was her passion.

"It's no different than kids wanting to take piano lessons. This is what I really want to do, I want to play basketball!" Janelle said.

She attended Brush College Elementary School in the west side of Salem. She was a strong-headed kid but not really outgoing. And once again, her mom wanted her to put on a dress now and them. She suggested she could wear shorts under the dress because she was so active in sports. Janelle and her mom squared a deal – to wear a dress once or twice a week.

During her grade school days her parents wanted her to be true to herself. They were worried that other kids might influence her to head in the wrong direction. Janelle was a leader-type person according to Brush College teachers. I don't think Paul and Earleen had much to worry about. She was going to be okay holding her own ground. She was just that type of person.

Janelle was highly respected among her peers and got along well with the student body. During the grade school days her best friend was Kelsey Huber. They did many things together and had each other's back. Kelsey played sports with Janelle. In fact, most of Janelle's friends were involved with sports.

"Janelle is the most caring friend I know. We did everything together. Playing sports with her through grade school and middle school was so much fun. I always knew that she would be the one to continue such a successful basketball career – she was so talented. I've been a supporter in her quest the entire time," Kelsey said.

Sometimes teachers can see the natural abilities and strengths in kids. Physical Education class in grade school was the place that the teacher recognized many things about Janelle.

"I remember Janelle in first grade. She was a caring girl but so aggressive that she would plow kids down just to get to the ball," said Loni Espinoza, her P.E. teacher.

Janelle started playing organized basketball at the Boys and Girls Club in the second grade. Her dad, Paul, played high school and college basketball in his days. He started working with his daughter – helping her with shooting form and other skills. He had very high expectation for Janelle. She was becoming quite the point guard with her ball-handling, passing, and shooting abilities.

By the time Janelle entered middle school she was playing with competitive traveling teams – Hotshots and then Team Concept both from Portland, Oregon. Team Concept was coached by Michael Abraham. She had also met Taylor, her boyfriend, who wasn't too crazy about basketball. His sport was lacrosse.

This was a very stressful situation for her, not only because her dad started pressuring her to do better on the court, but also because her boyfriend was not supportive of her dream. The time spent practicing, games, and the attention Janelle received took a toll on the relationship.

It was a bad situation altogether because Janelle's dad felt the boyfriend was a distraction to her and possibly keeping her from playing her best.

"What are you doing ... you need to pick up your D!" her dad yelled during one of the games.

Her dad's unacceptable behavior started when Janelle was in the sixth grade and continued through the seventh grade. She was doing her best and was only a child, but Paul would get so mad at her because she wasn't bringing her "A Game" every time.

During her seventh grade year, playing in a game with Team Concept, her coach Michael Abraham wasn't there. His brother Todd was coaching. Paul had been yelling at Janelle throughout the game. He got so angry that he walked over to Todd and talked to him for a bit. He then pulled Janelle out of the game and they left the gym.

On the drive back home, Janelle was very upset. Her dad was frustrated and angry. It was definitely an uncomfortable situation for her.

"You're embarrassing yourself out there. You're not playing up to par! I'm not going to let you play if you keep that up ... you need to pick up your game!" Paul yelled.

Janelle felt intense pressure and at times felt like quitting. She loved the game so much, but kept thinking, "Is this all really worth it?" She wanted to play high school and college basketball some day – that was her dream ... but at what cost?

Paul had opinions of Janelle's coaches and very high expectations from his daughter. His wife, Earleen, was feeling the stress level climb. It elevated to the point where she had to have a serious talk with her husband. They sat outside on their backyard deck. It was calm and quiet – a great time to talk.

"Paul, what are you doing? If you don't back off a little, you're going to lose her. Let her be a kid."

Paul started listening for the first time and decided to cooperate with what his wife was asking of him.

Janelle came really close to giving up her childhood dream. But luckily Paul started being more supportive and backed off. This helped the situation and Janelle was once again working harder than ever to become the best point guard she could be.

Her struggles with her boyfriend seemed to continue but she was managing things well. She was making things work because she was a pleaser and cared for him. Taylor was very supportive of Janelle in many things, but he never really liked the sport of basketball. To Janelle, other than her faith, basketball was what she lived and breathed.

It was a nightmare for Janelle, but she dealt with this holding her head up and continuing her quest. Basketball helped her deal with depressing things.

The basketball court was her counseling and her love. There was something about running the floor while dribbling the basketball that found a way to rest her mind. She was able to relax and block out issues that were going on in her life.

Janelle thought about what kind of things she could do to challenge herself. She practiced a lot day in and day out and played with several tournament teams.

When she got a well-deserved break, she watched players like Kyle Singler, Chris Paul, and Michael Jordon on tape. She picked up many skills by watching them play.

This young lady had a set of dribbling drills she practiced regularly on her own time. At night before bed, she would toss the basketball up in the air flipping her wrist and catching it as it came down – similarly to what Pistol Pete Maravich did. For some of you that might not know who the late Pistol Pete was, watch the movie *Pistol Pete*.

When Janelle began her quest at West Salem High School, she was a dominating point guard on the varsity team as a freshman. She was having a great time playing basketball at the high school level. The best part is that her parents were supporting her in what she loved doing.

"I love and adore my daughter – I would do anything for her. Whatever sacrifices I had to go through, I would do that for her in a second," Earleen said.

Mother and daughter were very close. They jogged together and participated in many indoor or outdoor activities. They once ran a half marathon together. Janelle would sign up for cycling classes in the off-season for strengthening and conditioning – her mom encouraged her. Her mom would even watch an NBA game with her now and then.

Things were going great and the family seemed to be at peace. But soon something was about to happen that would bring an uncomfortable storm about. The wonderful mother-daughter relationship would diminish severely.

After Janelle completed her freshman year at West High, her parents talked about moving her to Beaverton, Oregon. This city resides on the outskirts of Portland. They wanted the best for their daughter. If she played at Southridge High School, she would be playing with and against some of the top athletes in Oregon. Southridge was a powerhouse at the time. They played in the OSAA Metro League – one of the toughest leagues around. West Salem played in the CVC (Central Valley Conference), which was not as tough.

Their idea was that Janelle could play up to her full potential and improve her game against the best players. Initially Janelle did not want to go, but eventually she realized that this could be an opportunity for her to develop to her potential. College scouts would possibly take a look at her.

So the idea became a reality. Earleen and Paul would be living separately for the next two years. Janelle and her mom would rent an apartment in Beaverton while Paul would stay back in Salem.

During her sophomore year, Janelle was adapting to a new school. Earleen would wake up every morning, take her daughter to school, and drive back to Salem to give piano lessons. After the lessons she'd drive back to Beaverton to pick up Janelle from practice.

As time went on, Janelle discovered she was not happy at Southridge. Coach Michael Meek ran a disciplined slow-down offense – something she was not accustomed to. Janelle was a run-and-gun type of player that liked to attack the defense.

The coach moved her to the wing position – the two-guard. This did not go well with her and she found herself out of place in a powerhouse team that dominated girls' basketball.

The Southridge girls' basketball program was tough. They had 5:00 a.m. practices and weekend practices – comparable to college practices.

Once the season started, there was plenty of tension starting to develop among the players. Janelle was not playing point guard, which led to an unhappy experience for her.

Despite all of the frustrations with her parents and being moved to the wing position, she still held her head high and was proud of contributing to a successful season. Playing under Michael Meek was very difficult for her, but she did it.

Janelle was one of the leading scorers and played a huge role her sophomore year. With a talented squad, the Southridge Skyhawks went on to win the OSAA Oregon State Championship Title. That was a moment that Janelle and her parents will remember forever. They enjoyed watching the girls celebrate and tear down the opponent's net.

"It was a crazy feeling. Working so hard for that moment and achieving my goal. Making it all work in the end. All the hectic practices, days I didn't want to watch film, days I was exhausted, and times I didn't want to be in the gym for three hours. Saturday practices, weights, and plays I had to memorize. Everything was all worth it, being in that moment and in the spotlight – winning it all. To me, it was a feeling that was indescribable – we were state champions," Janelle said with a smile.

Moments like this don't come by too often for many families that wish the best for their kids. Wow, to be part of a state championship team that competes with the biggest schools in Oregon! That had to be a special moment for the Weiss family.

"We were all so happy for Janelle. Every parent dreams of an opportunity like this for their son or daughter. Just watching her help the team tear down the net after the game was full of mixed feelings. A lot of sacrifices and hard work went into this. But it was all worth it in the end," Earleen said.

When Janelle entered her junior year at Southridge, things got a little more depressing. The team acquired a new point guard that transferred from Westview High School, in Portland. She was a lot taller than Janelle and fit in with Michael Meek's slow-down offense. Janelle was hoping to take over the point-guard position her junior year – she found out different. She was once again playing the wing.

This caused tension on the team. There was more drama amongst the girls during the season. Janelle wanted to run the point-guard position and she wanted to fit into a faster-pace offense. She was out of place and felt like quitting.

Her parents encouraged her to stay and finish what she started. They felt that playing at Southridge was going to give her opportunities of possibly playing at a four-year college. Scouts were known to watch the tough high-school league she was in. Their daughter's dream was important to them and they were going to do the best to help her reach it.

"I'll finish out the season, but in the Spring I'm telling the coaches and my teammates that I'm going back to Salem," Janelle told her parents.

The wonderful mother-daughter relationship started to diminish. This was the time that Earleen felt the most distant from her daughter. The arguments and discussions went on throughout the year. Both parents were encouraging her to stay at Southridge. She finally gave in and finished her junior year there.

The Southridge Skyhawks made it past the first round of the playoffs, but were defeated in the second round by the Oregon City Pioneers.

When summer league came around, Janelle had already told the team and the coaches that she was not going to be returning for her senior year. Her parents once again tried to convince her to finish at Southridge, in fact, they really wanted her to play through the summer league there. Janelle was to the point of shutting down – very depressed.

There was a time where she just left the gym and no one could find her. She contacted the Athletic Director at West

Salem. She started making plans (on her own) to transfer back to West High – she was angry at her parents.

Her mom found her. Janelle was in her room downstairs. Earleen had a nice talk with her and some decisions were made.

"It just wasn't worth losing our daughter, we had to do what she was asking us to do," Earleen said.

Janelle had her parents deal with Head Coach Michael Meek. She was not about to go talk to him again about leaving his program. They did that and Janelle would soon be moving back to Salem.

She would once again be playing for Jason Unruh – the girls head basketball coach for the West Salem Titans. Jason was glad to get a top-notch point guard like Janelle – a player most teams would want. She had the ability to make her team better just by her presence. The other girls fed off of her energy and work ethic.

"Honestly, I was excited to be back in my hometown where I grew up. I was homesick and I missed a lot of my friends from here, my Assistant Coach Em, my soccer coach, Tom Jaeger, and all my soccer friends. They were always so supportive and sweet. I was just excited to be able to graduate with all the kids I grew up with and loved," Janelle said.

It was so strange for her to be gone two years and then return. She realized that because she was a freshman when she played varsity, most of her basketball teammates were gone. It was a new team at West High and Janelle had to find a way to fit in – she did not know what to expect.

One of her best friends, Whitney Ferrin, was not playing basketball anymore. Janelle was disappointed. Sometimes life throws unexpected things at us. Whitney was one of Janelle's best friends growing up. She assumed Whitney would be playing basketball – at least there would be one girl she knew on the team. But it wasn't the case.

During the years 2009-2010, her senior year, Janelle was a force playing the point-guard position on the varsity team. The talent surrounding her was lacking a little, but to her it was more important to be happy playing the game she loved in her hometown.

Janelle developed a great player-coach relationship with assistant coach, Jesse Ailstock. He helped her improve her game in all areas. She had no clue that Jesse was eyeing a head coach position for the Chemeketa Community College Women's Basketball Team.

At the end of her high school basketball season Janelle helped her team make it to the playoffs. They were eliminated and did not make it to the state tournament. She had completed an unusual path toward a successful basketball career in high school. Playing for the West Salem Titans her senior year, she averaged 16.6 points, 2.6 assists, and 1.6 steals. Her field-goal percentage was 47.3%, 3-point percentage was 38.6%, and her free-throw percentage was 80%. She earned two awards, 1st Team All-League CVC and 1st Team All-Region.

It was time for decisions about where Janelle would play college basketball. Several four-year colleges expressed interest, George Fox University and Oregon State University were two that Janelle visited on recruiting trips. Earleen and Paul did everything they could to put their daughter in a position to reach her dream – to play at a Division I, Division II, or Division III college.

One of Janelle's goals was to graduate college debt free. She is a very conscientious person – definitely not a procrastinator. She takes her school work very serious. She understood that in college the grades were very important. You can't play basketball without passing grades.

After returning from a recruiting trip at George Fox University in Newberg, Oregon, it seemed as if Janelle was interested in playing there.

"George Fox would have been such a great fit for her. It was a Christian College – a great fit because of her faith. I felt she would be safe there and it would be a four-year school," Earleen said.

Janelle received a call from Jesse Ailstock. He asked her if she had signed with anyone yet. Janelle thought highly of Jesse. She was also thinking of playing time as a college freshman. At a university there were no guarantees – the competition would be much tougher.

When Jesse expressed interest in her coming to Chemeketa Community College, well, things got much easier for Janelle to make a decision of where she would be playing college basketball. This would give her the opportunity to stay in her hometown. She could develop more to be ready for the Division I level in two years.

That decision did not go well with her parents – they were disappointed and felt she was a better player than at the community college level.

"What! Are you joking Janelle?" Earleen was surprised, "You are much better than the girls at Chemeketa, and I don't feel Chemeketa is a safe place for you to be."

But Janelle felt that playing for Jesse is what was going to make her happy. His style of coaching and the ideas he had for her to grow as a point guard was convincing enough. So her parents finally gave in and supported Janelle on her decision.

Parents want what's best for their kids, but sometimes it's best to allow the kids to decide what's best for them.

"I just wanted Janelle to be safe. I wanted her to experience the campus life at a Christian College. You only get one shot – I just wanted the best for her," Earleen said.

In 2010, Janelle signed with the Chemeketa Community College Storm. The women's basketball program would be getting one of the best point guards in the state for two seasons. Jesse Ailstock was so happy to hear that she was going to be playing for him. He thought very highly of Janelle and would do anything to protect her at Chemeketa.

Janelle's first year at Chemeketa was frustrating. Although she played the point-guard position she did not take many shots. There were a group of girls that had already been in the program previous to Janelle coming in. It was tough for Jesse to build an offense that executed efficiently. This ended in a losing season for the Chemeketa Storm.

Along with a losing season, was the end of the relationship Janelle had with her boyfriend, Taylor. It wasn't going to work. Basketball was Janelle's love and the dream of playing Division I basketball was still in her vision. Taylor was not supportive of basketball, so the two went their separate ways.

With all those issues going on, Janelle had another distraction having to do with her brother – it affected her emotionally. Earleen says that due to bullying, teasing, and other things, Eric got involved with drugs and eventually into some trouble. It's tough to see a family member dealing with such an uncomfortable situation. He checked in and out of rehabilitation centers to deal with his addiction.

At the beginning of her college sophomore year Janelle faced another obstacle. During practices and games she was experiencing excruciating pain in her knees and feet. Despite the pain, she was helping the team in many areas, points, assists, and steals – she was doing very well.

It was early in the preseason and the coaches were doing whatever they could to help her play through the pain. They tried physical therapy, stretching, taping, etc. Nothing seemed to be working. The pain continued each day – it got worse.

"She was too young to be having all of those problems. I told Janelle that we had to take her to Portland to see a podiatrist," Earleen said.

Janelle sat out for a few weeks and came down with a heavy depression. She again questioned herself if this was all worth it. Her Christian faith was solid and she started thinking about moving to Montana. That's where Steven, her brother, was doing mission work. He was involved with YWAM (Youth with a Mission).

Earleen wasn't about to let her daughter give up a dream of playing basketball in college – they had put too much work and sacrifice into the whole thing. She set up appointments with an orthopedic surgeon, podiatrist, and a physical therapist. She also set up an MRI for Janelle.

In a few weeks they finally found out what the problem was. An orthopedic specialist discovered that Janelle's feet were flat. She needed orthotics to fit the shape of her feet. The knees were taking punishment as well because of this condition.

She started wearing the orthotics that the orthopedic specialist recommended. In addition, the therapist worked out the scar tissue in the knee. She started feeling some relief and the healing began. Janelle started working her way back to recovery.

"I about gave up on my dream, but looking back, I always knew in the back of my mind that I would fight through the pain and persevere," Janelle said.

When she reached the point of playing her best, Jesse Ailstock used her to help his team win games. They had a group of girls that worked well together – the execution was amazing.

Chemeketa played in the NWAACC Southern Region. Janelle was doing an amazing job running the point-guard position – the number one spot. In one game they traveled to Eugene, Oregon. They were visiting Lane Community College. Lane C.C. had not lost a game in a very long time – they had a winning streak going.

When the game ended, Janelle led all scorers with a game high of 27 points. Her teammates did a phenomenal job defensively and offensively – she would want to give them all the credit in the world. They defeated Lane and spoiled their winning streak.

In another game against Umpqua Community College, Janelle got into a zone. Her teammates were feeding her the ball and she was hitting all the shots she was taking. She was making shots from 3-point land, from the free throw line, and driving to the bucket. She was dishing out assists and making steals. It was one of the highlights of her last year at Chemeketa. She led all scorers with a game high of 30 points.

"Janelle is a huge blessing in our life. I speak for my husband and myself. To have her as our daughter makes us both very proud," her mom said.

Before the playoffs got going in the post season, Janelle received a call from Jordan Green, the assistant coach at the University of Idaho.

Janelle Weiss, a Determined Athlete

"Hey this is Jordan Green – I'm calling from the University of Idaho. We want you to know that we are super interested in your playing style. We need a point guard for next season. My boss and I are going to come out to one of your games and hopefully your playoff tournament. We would love to meet with you and set up a time for a visit."

Janelle was ecstatic! I mean someone from a Division I school wanted her. This was her dream she had worked so hard for. But first she had to take care of business and finish post play for Chemeketa.

This young lady helped the Storm to a 21-8 record advancing to the NWAACC Championships in Kennewick, Washington. The team ended a successful season placing fourth at the tournament. She averaged 17.5 points, 4.1 assists, and 3.5 rebounds – not bad for a 5' 5" point guard. She was named the 2011-2012 NWAACC Southern Region Player of the Year – a well-earned award. That award goes along with the many others she received throughout her basketball career.

At Chemeketa, she was involved in a scholars program which required maintaining a GPA that was above average.

Janelle made her teammates better and they all respected her and followed her lead on the floor. Janelle gives credit to her entire team for the support and for being a family to her while she was at Chemeketa.

The Chemeketa Storm ... Marissa Angulo, Guard; KayLynne Kuenzi, Guard; Kaitlin Counts, Guard; Chantee Stanton, Guard; Lauren Codling, Post; Carly Bull, Guard; Crystal Van Huffel, Post; Kim VanKyke, Post; Hannah Frederick, Guard; Jordan Klebaum, Guard; Jesse Ailstock, Head Coach; Matt Olson, Assistant Coach; Natasha Crisman, Assistant Coach; Carrie Garrison, Assistant Coach; Carlos Navarro, Manager.

"She's a proven winner who brought competitiveness and efficiency to practices and games, which rubbed off on our other kids," Jesse Ailstock said.

When Janelle's chapter was completed at Chemeketa, she started working more hours at Jamba Juice. She then worked for Tan Republic – two local stores at different times. She liked buying clothes and enjoyed doing other things in life. Her responsibility nature demonstrated that she wasn't going to rely on her parents for extra money. She also did some babysitting for Jesse and Janet Ailstock on occasions. She had a great relationship with her coach and his wife.

The decision process of what four-year college to attend was taking the surface again and Janelle had to make a decision from several colleges that were interested in her. Head Coach Jon Newlee from the University of Idaho was looking for another point guard. That was the missing link that would make his team strong in the WAC Conference. He liked the way Janelle played and knew she could be an asset to his basketball program.

It didn't take long for Janelle to decide after visiting the University of Idaho. She felt comfortable with the coaching staff and she felt like her style of play would fit the program. And most importantly, she was going to be used as a point guard.

On April 17th, 2012, Janelle signed a letter of intent to play basketball at the University of Idaho, in Moscow, Idaho. She became an Idaho Vandal. Her energy, ball handling, diving for basketballs, competitiveness, shooting, defense, and more had earned her a chance to compete with Krissy Karr – a returning point guard that started for several games last season for the Vandals.

Signing a letter of intent to play college basketball for a Division I College may not mean a lot to some people. But when you've just learned what Janelle Weiss went through to reach her dream, well, you might just think a little differently. There are sacrifices, politics, hard work, injuries, financial need, family support, and the list goes on and on. I call Janelle Weiss a northwest success story.

"What makes me happy is when people look up to me, especially the young kids. I would love to be a role model for young kids. I'm not afraid to state my opinion – I'm a competitor but caring at the same time," Janelle said.

Janelle loves her parents. They have gone through so much together as a family. Things can get very tough at times – you go through adversity. Through the process we all learn many things as the Weiss family did.

"Both my parents have been supportive. My dad was more when I was younger. He pushed me to the highest level and wanted me to be better than good. My mom has always been there for me. She cares so much for me – would do anything for us kids. She attends all my games and is always cheering for my team," Janelle said.

Janelle is already thinking about her future. She wants to help the University of Idaho make it to the NCAA Tournament – March Madness. She also wants to help her teammates achieve their goals. Playing professional basketball overseas is another thing on her mind. And then beyond that, she would love to become a sports broadcaster. She admires Erin Andrews, a famous broadcaster. And lastly she would love to have a family someday – setting a good example for her kids.

Can't is Not an Option for Alex Hurlburt

To have a missing body part can be a disadvantage to someone that allows it. People engage to the person that looks different – it's human nature. An observer staring and whispering, "Wonder what happened to him?" ... "That poor kid I feel bad for him." I'm sure many other comments – the list goes on and on. This can do something to the inner soul and the self esteem of a young boy. One would imagine this being a tough ordeal to go through while attending elementary and middle school.

I had the pleasure of sitting down with an amazing young boy who overcame so many things – a kid with positive character and a perfectionist attitude. By the middle of the interview I had forgotten that he had a missing limb. It was no surprise to me when I watched him play catcher for the West Salem JBO Titans – an all-star baseball team.

Alex Hurlburt was born on September 8, 2000, in Portland, Oregon. He is the son of Gerald (Ed), and Julia (Julie). He also has a brother, Sean, who is four years older.

When Julie was pregnant with Alex, Ed drove her to get an ultrasound – a procedure that allows the doctor to see the baby inside the womb. After the procedure was completed, the doctor didn't want to say anything negative. The parents asked if everything was okay with the baby, but the doctor was hesitant to say anything. The Hurlburts knew something was not quite right. They finally dragged it out of the doctor. They were told that the baby's left arm (below the elbow) was missing.

"I remember the ultrasound because it was take-your-child-to-work day. Because the procedure was taking too long, many things went through my head. He's our son it should be no big deal. But then my conscience kept telling me, is there something else wrong with him? It was a real shock – I was very emotional," Julie said.

Ed was stunned in disbelief – like the entire world collapsed on him. He walked out to his car and fell apart – it was very emotional for him as well. They were both torn inside – their baby was going to be born with a defect.

A few days went by and they started adjusting to the unpredictable future. The curiosity of what might have caused this drove them to do more research.

They thought about getting another opinion to find out what might have caused this to their son, who wasn't even born yet. Could it have been that Julie was a little older? She thought maybe that was a factor.

It was more likely that amniotic band syndrome was the case. A congenital birth defect believed to be caused by entrapment of fetal parts – a limb or digits in fibrous amniotic bands in utero. In other words, before the baby was born, some of the parts were caught and entangled. Another possibility was that loose strands could have wrapped around his arm and caused a lack of blood circulation – a vascular incident. But it's difficult to know what exactly caused Alex's defect.

There was another problem discovered by the doctor. His feet appeared to be turned inside. The ultrasound was a living nightmare for the family.

Julie had dreams at night which were very unpleasant. She dreamt of her son having other things wrong with him – it was stressful for her.

"It was very difficult to understand why this happened to our son. Would he be able to make friends? How will he fit in at school? Many thoughts came to me relating to a young kid's self esteem. It just didn't seem fair to our little boy," she said.

Could there be anything positive about this situation? Julie says that because of the ultrasound, they knew what to expect. It gave them time to prepare for his birth. They were also able to do research on how to treat his feet. It wouldn't be as much of a shock to them seeing their newborn child. They would love him no matter what.

On the flipside, she was very worried about Alex's health. She couldn't predict the feature, but was ready to face it. That's something she thought about and accepted the fact. She would have to make that adjustment. Alex was her child and nothing would keep her from loving him.

"If we could take back how we felt about Alex, we would in a second. The way things have turned out, we couldn't be more proud," Ed said.

A few months later, in the morning, Julie's water broke. The due date was still five weeks away. Julie sensed that something was wrong. She was taken by ambulance to St. Vincent's Hospital in Portland. Alex was born prematurely into this world.

Despite all, Alex passed the Apgar scores with flying colors. Apgar score (Appearance, Pulse, Grimace, Activity, and Respiration) was developed by Virginia Apgar in 1952.

This test is usually given to a baby at one minute after birth and again at five minutes after birth.

After three days at the hospital the Hurlburts brought home a healthy baby boy – a new addition to the family.

"I remember that day, I stayed home from work. I was so worried about the baby – it was very difficult for me to focus," Ed said.

As Alex started growing, his parents learned of ways to treat his feet. They would massage them in certain ways. That seemed to help improve his condition. They were given instructions on all kinds of therapy. They could help treat Alex at home.

"I just wanted to be able to play catch with my son, something any dad would want. I wasn't asking for anything much more," Ed said.

At six months old, Alex started attending the West Salem Kids Care. This was a daycare that the Hurlburts took their son to on their way to work. Nancy Mueller was the daycare provider for Alex. She enjoyed Alex for nine years. She speaks very highly of the Hurlburts.

According to Nancy, in his toddler years at the daycare, he was very shy. That didn't change the fact that he was a happy child. He was always smiling. As he grew older, year by year, he became familiar with all of the kids there – he started feeling safe and secure.

Somehow it was destined that he would be a great athlete. As a one year-old kid, during playtime, Nancy threw a rubber ball at him. Alex caught it! Most kids that age (with two arms) could not do that.

By the time he was old enough to understand how other kids at the daycare viewed him, things started changing for him. Some of the kids started asking about Alex's arm. They knew that he was physically different – they were reacting as any young child would.

Nancy decided to educate them on why Alex was like that. She read a book with the kids that helped explain how Alex was born with a defect. He's not any different and is just as normal as any of us. The book was an excellent resource that answered their questions. The entire daycare adapted well. They were all nice to Alex and made him feel comfortable.

The daycare has been such a blessing to Alex's life. This facility helped Alex develop his social skills. The more time he spent there the more comfortable he became. The group of kids there became his friends – that was a comfort zone for him.

During daycare, Alex struggled with activities that required the use of two hands. Cutting a piece of paper is one example. One day, Nancy was having the kids cut out a picture from a magazine. They were to paste them all together into one huge picture – a team project. Alex found a way to accomplish this task. He would use his short limb to position the picture and then cut it holding the scissors in his right hand. Then he would turn the picture with his right hand and repeat the process all over again. He discovered a way that worked for him.

Another task was tying his shoes. Nancy had some wooden shoes for the kids to practice on. She called the exercise "The Wooden Shoe Practice." Alex was slower than all of the kids due to the use of one hand, but he figured out a way to accomplish that challenge.

There were many more things he had to figure out how to do. It was a tremendous lift having Nancy there to encourage him and guide him on whatever he needed.

"It was a real joy being around Alex, his determination was amazing! Kids would tell him that he couldn't play baseball – well he hit the baseball very well. They also said he couldn't play goalie in soccer. He was an excellent goalie," Nancy said.

One time there were two new kids that came into the daycare. They didn't know Alex – they started teasing him. "Hey look at him with that one arm!" Alex was feeling hurt and didn't know how to handle the situation. He went to Nancy for comfort and advice. She gave him a hug.

"What's wrong Alex?"
"Those kids are teasing me about my arm."

Nancy established an area she calls "The Peace Table." When there was an issue, she served as the mediator for the kids. She brought the two boys and Alex together for a meeting at the table. Nancy had Alex explain to the boys what happened to him. He told them about how he was born like that. They discussed things and arrived at a resolution. Knowledge about something can be powerful. The Peace Table worked. The two kids treated Alex with the upmost respect after that.

"Alex is an amazing child. He's smart and can figure out how to do just about anything. He's a go-get-it type of kid with great confidence. His entire family is such a joy. His brother Sean also attended my daycare. Alex is a kid that everyone at the daycare will always remember. We love him and will also try to keep in touch with him and his family," Nancy said.

At three and a half years old, Alex started catching the baseball. He would catch the ball, remove his mitt by tucking it under his short limb, grab the baseball with his right hand, and throw it back to his dad. Alex was the type of kid that wanted his art to be perfect. He worked hard every day to improve his speed in catching the baseball and throwing it back to his dad.

Ed's endless hours teaching him about baseball gave him assurance that he could be a baseball player. Alex is forever grateful to his dad. Ed put the time in to give his son the opportunity to be the best he could be at baseball – a caring father. They have a great father-son relationship.

"My dad got me started on playing baseball. He does so many things for me. He's always trying to help me build up my muscles. It's always a challenge building up the shoulder muscle where I don't have an arm. If I need anything, he's always there for me. I'm truly thankful for everything he's done," Alex said.

Balance had always been a problem while trying to accomplish physical tasks. The body doesn't carry the same weight on each side. Ed was always trying to find ways to develop his muscles on the short-limb side. Alex would sit on a kitchen chair and all of a sudden just fall down. He was falling down several times through the years as he learned how to balance himself – it was an adjustment he had to make. He was the type of kid that would learn quickly to adapt to his physical condition.

Ed and Julie learned very quickly to not allow their son to say "I can't" around their house. It just wasn't an option. Ed felt that saying those words was a cop-out and it ticked him off. He saw what his son was capable of – he was going to encourage him to succeed at anything he desired.

Alex visited the Shriners (a children's hospital in Portland) once a year to see if there was a prosthetic that he might be able to use – they seem to come up with new discoveries from year to year. Each visit was useless. He seemed to reject everything – Alex was comfortable without assistance.

Alex dealt with different types of discomfort. Kids would stare, tease, and point at him. He would not respond to negative people. He'd keep everything inside and was very quiet in the evenings – a young boy that abandoned himself from the cruel world. Sometimes there were moments of torture. Kids would follow him around and stare. Some were mean and others just curious.

Julie notices to this day that people of all ages still stare and whisper wherever they go. It used to bother her more, but as time went by she was able to deal with it better.

Brush College Elementary School was the starting point of major challenges – this is in addition to the daycare challenges. He would face new kids and adults he was not familiar with.

We all have an idea of how difficult it was to start school in the beginning. Well, just imagine how much tougher it was for Alex. Kids can be cruel, but at the same time kids can be nice. One of Alex's best friends to this day is Noah Juarez. Noah started playing sports with Alex at a very young age. This made the school days easier – he had a best friend.

During P.E. class Alex was at the top of the group as far as athletics. He worked hard to prove to everyone he was just as normal. If he couldn't do something, he had those words in the back of his mind, "Can't is not an option." He would find a way through strong will.

"He was one of my most athletic kids. He never complained – always found a way to adapt – very persistent at anything and never gave up. He was somewhat of a perfectionist. If a skill was difficult he would practice until he mastered it," said Loni Espinoza, his P.E. teacher.

Speaking of difficult challenges, there was this competition held in P.E. once a year. It was called "The Dairy Queen Challenge." The students had one week to make an attempt at this challenge. If any kid could climb the thick rope up to the ceiling (using hands but no feet) they earned a Dairy Queen Blizzard. Keep in mind we're talking about a grade school gym and not a high school gym.

Alex set a mark for this challenge. In all fairness, Loni always wanted every kid in class to have the opportunity to succeed. She allowed Alex to use one hand and his toes. Alex was so excited about the opportunity to climb the rope for a blizzard. He practiced hard all week at mastering a technique to do this. He placed the rope between the toes as he reached up with one hand to pull himself up. Step by step he climbed the rope.

When it was time for the challenge, thirty kids in his class were competing. Only five students completed the challenge – Alex was one of the kids. The other kids were, Roman Ganchenko, Jaiden Holder, Kassidy Jones, and Samantha Payne.

There was a student in the class that wasn't too happy about it. He seemed to think that it wasn't fair because Alex could use his toes.

The teacher explained, "I'll tell you what … if you can climb the rope using one hand and your toes, you'll get a blizzard."

The student that complained hopped onto the rope and started climbing using his feet and one hand. He couldn't even make it one foot up the rope. This qualified the adjustment the teacher made. It was probably tougher to climb the rope the way Alex did it. This young man worked much harder than anyone to achieve this challenge. He mastered the skill.

Alex found himself being pretty popular amongst his peers. He had friends in school – even a few girls that expressed interest. He was adjusting well in grade school taking a day at a time.

He remembers a time when he was following a group of kids. They climbed over a tall fence. One of the boys turned around and laughed at Alex.

"You can't climb that fence – don't even try ... ha-ha!"

Once again, Alex had those words in his mind, "Can't is not an option."

He hopped on the fence and started climbing using his one hand and two feet. He struggled a little, but his determination and fight to prove the kid wrong was an inspiring sight that would have been nice to see. While the boys watched him get over the fence, they took a big swallow feeling stupid. After that ordeal, the boys became his friends. He gained their respect by defying the odds.

A sense of humor started becoming natural to Alex – he was that comfortable being who he was. One day the P.E. teacher was warning the kids not to take the soccer balls out of the barrel. She had about 30 soccer balls that were supposed to be left alone. The teacher was unaware of her sarcastic talk to the kids, and realized too late. She was meaning it as a joke.

"If anyone else takes another ball from the barrel, I'll cut their arm off!"

Alex responded, "You better listen to her, look what she did to me!"

That definitely caught all of the kids' attention ... they left the soccer balls alone. The teacher felt bad and apologized to Alex, but he knew it wasn't directed at him – he just played along with her joking threat.

His grades were very good. He always wanted to do the best he could in his school work. Being so competitive, he worked hard on his assignments. He would often ask for extra math problems to do. Math was his favorite subject by far.

Julie says that he is a sensitive-caring child. She remembers having a bad day at the office. Some stressful things had happened. Being a parole officer can be a challenging job from time to time ... or maybe all the time. Alex did something that touched her heart and brought her to tears.

He had written a journal at school. She somehow found it and read it. He mentioned being worried about his mom's day at the job. And that no one loved his mom as much as he did. All the things she goes through at work, and then coming home and taking care of him – supporting him in whatever he might need. That meant so much to him.

"Mom has taken so much time off work to be there for me. I'm very lucky to have a mom like her," said Alex.

He was a boy that was involved in many activities during school. He was chosen to be in a leadership role called "Peace Makers" at Brush College Elementary. This was a program developed for kids to help other kids solve issues during recess. In addition, he once had the responsibility of being a tour guide to the new students coming in – showing them the entire school.

Alex was a member of "Bouncers," a grade school jump-rope club. The teacher had customized a rope he used.

He became fairly good at jumping rope – he was participating very well in the club.

"We made a custom rope for him. It was made to tie above his left elbow. He would use his right arm to swing the rope – he mastered the technique well," said his P.E. teacher.

During the spring, the kids were performing a jump-rope show at a different grade school. This was an annual event at the end of the school year. At the assembly there was a kindergarten teacher that saw Alex. She immediately walked over to Loni, the P.E. teacher. She explained that one of her students was just like Alex – same missing arm. After the assembly, Loni went over to Alex.

"Alex, there's a teacher here that wants to know if you could talk to one of her students. The student has a missing arm just like you. Would you be willing to do that?"
"Oh! I'd love to do that," Alex said.

He inspires other kids, and he takes great pride and joy in helping any kid that might have the same struggles he once did.

In any team he played for he was always trying to encourage his teammates. If they made a mistake on the field, he'd talk to them and cheer them up – a great lift.

Alex thinks about helping others. If there's something he can help them with he's always willing to make that effort – he knows so much because of his experiences as a young boy.

Certainly we can admit that Alex will face the impossible at one time or another. But is that really true? Let's take music for example.

"If I could possibly do that – why wouldn't I try? I've always wanted to play trombone. I worked as hard as I could to hold it up. I realized it wasn't going to work out. I didn't let that stop me from playing an instrument. I switched to the baritone – a mini tuba. I found a way to do what I like. I think about working harder each time until I find a way to accomplish that task," Alex explains.

Elana Pena, a lady who Julie met through her boss, has a son like Alex – same arm missing from the elbow down. Vidal was an outstanding wrestler in his time. He attended Central High School in Independence, Oregon. Vidal inspired Alex to start doing sports. His successful experiences despite his defect were great examples. Alex met with him about three times and learned many things from him. Alex even tried wrestling for two years – he decided it wasn't his sport.
Vidal is the one that showed Alex how to tie his shoes with one hand more efficiently. That has to be a huge challenge for anyone. Alex had built great confidence in himself with just the few times he met with Vidal. He thought about how Vidal accomplished so many things in the sport he loved. There was no reason he couldn't find success in many things life threw at him.
Alex's dad, Ed, picked up on many things his son showed an interest in throughout the years. One time, when Alex was four years old, they were at a store looking at toys. Alex gets on this three-wheel scooter and starts riding it. Then, at seven years old it was a razor scooter. His balance was off and he struggled a little but that didn't bother him. They bought the scooter and brought it home. Ed took the handlebars from a mountain bike and attached them to the scooter. This allowed Alex to hold on with his short limb and to balance himself more efficiently.

As Alex grew older he became a self-motivated kid that tackled most obstacles that came his way. He wanted to learn how to ride a bike. His dad built an attachment-platform on one of the handlebars. This made it easier for him to adjust and the balance became much better. He learned how to ride a bike. Once again, his parents were going to make sure that he had the opportunity to do whatever he wanted.

Ron Juarez has been a mentor to Alex since his first-grade year. He coached him in three sports, football, basketball, and baseball. He helped Alex realize the potential he had to succeed in sports.

He loves football, basketball, and baseball. Alex played football for a Boys and Girls Club team. Hitting someone takes great pleasure in his mind. At home he enjoys playing football with his older brother, Sean ... he says he loves tackling him. Alex played defensive end for his team. One of the football coaches once said that Alex was the best defensive player on the team – and one of the best in the league.

Alex is also a basketball player. He has great form in shooting the basketball. His challenges are going left and passing left. He has worked hard to make a pass to his left. Many would see his passes as being fancy – behind the back. Sometimes he would use his right hand and pass the ball between his legs.

He adapts well and is persistent. Since basketball is my favorite sport, I had the pleasure of showing him a few ways he could pass to his left with his right arm. Needless to say, he picked it up really quick.

He played basketball in the Boys and Girls Club League during grade school. The coaches would come down on kids that tried to pass the ball like Alex did. They made it perfectly clear to the other players, that only one player could make those fancy-looking passes. They tried to teach fundamentals, but with Alex, there had to be an exception.

Although he loves football and basketball, his real dream sport is in the diamond. Alex began playing baseball in an organized little league when he was five years old. His natural instincts and hard work paid off. He played catcher, outfielder, pitcher, and first base ... oh, and did I mention he can really hit the baseball? Coach Ron Juarez talked highly of Alex and treated him no different than any other member on the team.

"I've known Alex since his kindergarten year. He's a fearless competitor. He thinks he has two hands and doesn't see it any different – it's great to have him on our team," Ron said.

Over the years, Ed and Ron helped Alex with technique on all three sports. Swinging a bat, proper stance, or catching the baseball. In football, Ron always told Alex that he had to get lower when he ran with the ball. He made Alex do the drills over and over until he got it right. Alex was willing and improved with Ron's instruction.

Alex played Triple-A baseball, which is a junior league – a step away from youth major league. As a nine year-old, Alex tried out for the major league. Ed remembers the tryouts. Alex was in the outfield. When the fly ball came his way, he made a spectacular-diving catch that caught the coaches' attention. There weren't too many nine year-olds that could make a play like that.

When he plays catcher, he does an amazing job. Try to visualize this, he catches the baseball with the glove in his right hand as it comes zooming, removes his mitt with the ball in it, tucks it under his short limb, grabs the baseball with his right hand, and throws it to the pitcher or a baseman. It's like watching the gears on an automatic transmission. He does this faster than some kids can grab the ball from their own glove using both hands. His batting form and swing are precise. His stance is square and he holds the bat like any player would. You won't even notice that he has a missing arm by the way he waits for the ball to be pitched – truly amazing.

After playing baseball for one season, this young man had developed some skills that were noticeable. Ron Juarez, his mentor and coach for football, basketball and baseball, walked up to his parents. He asked them if Alex could join his all-star baseball team – a traveling team.

Ed and Julie were surprised. Did Ron feel sorry for Alex? Was he doing this just to be nice? They begin to wonder. Ron explained to them that Alex had some real talent and his team could really use him.

"We were like, really! To hear what Ron said about our son was such a great feeling. We felt overjoyed and very proud," Ed said.

Both parents agree on a favorite highlight moment with their son. When Alex was ten years old, he was playing with the Oregon Select traveling team. He knocked one over the fence – his first homerun! Everyone went crazy! Alex ran the bases with a smile on his face. When he ran over home plate, all of his teammates cleared the bench to come celebrate with him.

"We were so proud of our son. It was unbelievable to experience a moment like that, to actually see the accomplishment. He worked so hard for this and it made us feel very happy for him – a special moment," said Julie.

There were times during games where the umpire or even an opponent would give Alex that look. It was like a feel-sorry look that his parents had learned to recognize. Oh, this kid can't play. He only has one arm. After Alex hits the baseball or makes a double play, well, I think they start showing a little respect. They realize what he's capable of.

In game three of the Triple Crown Fall Nationals in Las Vegas, Alex was playing first base. He caught a line drive and made a double play. He also pitched a three-inning no hitter.

Another play he made that had the crowd on their feet was when he was playing catcher. He caught a foul ball and threw it all the way to second base for a double play.

There were times when Alex struggled in games – he even went on some hitting slumps. He has such high expectations for himself. When things don't go so well, he comes down on himself and feels bad.

"We tell Alex that nobody expects him to hit a homerun every time. It's okay to not have an A game all the time," said his mom.

Ed is great about talking to Alex after games and evaluating what might have caused some of the errors. But what's even better, is that he always talks about the great things accomplished during the game. That helps his son calm down and to also realize that he isn't perfect – and that's okay because no one's perfect.

Alex has never had any kind of conflict with any of his teammates. The only kind would have to be the competitiveness. There might be another kid that's battling for the same position. Sometimes kids want to be better than someone else at hitting or fielding, etc. Resentment might have taken place from teammates if Alex was getting more attention due to his circumstance. The coaches never gave Alex any kind of special treatment. They were fair to all of them based on skill level.

Coaches mentioned that Alex was one of the best outfielders in the state for his age-group. That takes some doing. A future for this kid is in the making. With his hard work and perseverance he could go a very long way.

In the year 2012, Alex was ready to enter Straub Middle School – the school district had just built it. This school enrolled sixth, seventh, and eighth graders. He was a little nervous about facing a new set of teachers, students, and administration. He had a talk with his mom. They both agreed on him going with a friend for the first day.

When Alex arrived at the school, he found that things were much better than he expected. There were no seventh or eighth graders there the first day. This was planned to make it easier for the incoming sixth graders.

During the fall season, Alex felt comfortable being in middle school. He says that no one has really treated him bad. The only thing that bothered him at times was the rumors that would start, but just everyday stuff – it had nothing to do with his arm.

He feels that because of the bullying policies, most kids think before they make fun of anyone in a cruel way. A student could get expelled and possibly sent to a special school away from the public school system.

While attending a larger school than he was accustomed to, some different challenges would arise. Interacting with teachers, playing the tuba, and making new friends were some challenges.

It didn't take him long to overcome those challenges. He likes his band teacher, Jaimie Hall. They figured out a way that Alex could play the tuba. Holding the tuba up used to be a problem, not to mention carrying it to school and back.

He was stronger in middle school – this enabled him to hold it up better. They also bought another tuba to keep at home. One instrument would stay at the school and the other at home. He would not need to carry it back and forth – great solution.

Alex takes great pride in being part of a band that performs in school concerts – a rewarding experience.

Language Arts is another subject he really enjoys. Casey McConville has taught him so many ways to improve his writing. He was able to fight through his shyness and interacted with several teachers – something he was struggling with early in the school year.

"One of my favorite teachers is Theresa Norris – she's my P.E. teacher," Alex said.

As the days went by, he felt more comfortable with the environment. Initiating conversation with other kids was always difficult for him. He sometimes felt a little insecure. But with his positive character he was able to overcome that – he improved every day.

In addition to Noah Juarez and Ryan Stebner, Alex made some good friends that became close to him. His new friends were, Simon Thompson, Zach Cones, Sebastian Deleon, Gabe Anderson, Julia Conley, Monica Mendoza, and Ella Albee.

"School is fun this year, much better than I expected. I really enjoy being around my friends," Alex said.

The sports world was becoming part of Alex's life. He was finding a love for all three sports, football, basketball, and baseball. In middle school, he was also thinking about adding track and field.

He played football for the Jets, a Boys and Girls Club 110 lbs. weight league. Seventh graders could be in this league as well, but they couldn't weigh more than 95 lbs.

Alex played several positions for his team. On defense he played guard and tackle. On offense he played running back and wide receiver. He helped the Jets by scoring ten touchdowns, assisting in 25 tackles (6 on his own), and playing a lot of minutes.

This year he plans on playing basketball for a new league called SKEF (Salem/Keizer Education Foundation). In the previous years he played in the Skyball League in Salem, Oregon.

"My parents have set such a great example for me. They both have good jobs. Dad's a sales manager and Mom's a parole officer. But I want to play college baseball and then become a professional baseball player. If that doesn't work out, I would like to work in the sports medicine area. I want to be able to help people in the sports world," Alex said.

Ed and Julie have some advice for other parents that might have a son or daughter like Alex.

"Encourage your kids. Never lead on that they can't do something. Appreciate the fact if you know beforehand that something is wrong physically. It prepares you for so much – it makes things easier. Don't put any preconceived notions in your head that things aren't going to work out. Try not to worry about the "what ifs." Sometimes support networks are more for the parents than the kid. Give your child every opportunity to accomplish what he or she wants – the results can surprise you," Ed said and Julie agreed.

There are certain people that have an impact on lives of others. These people go out of their way to help others and to enrich them with positive values.

"We owe so much to two people that I can think of, Ron Juarez and Nancy Mueller. They have been a great help to our son. We are so thankful for those two," Ed said.

Alex plans to continue his music and sports career – he is working hard every day. Someday he will have the opportunity to possibly play football, basketball, or baseball for the West Salem High School Titans. And then, he could possibly play in college. It will be such a great accomplishment in his resume. Go Alex!

GRAYSON BOUCHER

Little guys, Landon and Grayson

Grayson and his dad Steve

Grayson and his mom Molly

Started shooting baskets on an indoor hoop

Photographs

Molly and her two boys

Grayson and Landon

Grade school days

Middle school days

Photographs

Matt Espinoza (Noza), Grayson (Professor), Jake Espinoza (Kid Espi)

Hometown friend, Matt, hanging out with the Professor

The Professor – Grayson Boucher Plus More NW Sports Stories

Professor is from the NW, Salem/Kiezer in Oregon

**Molly, Grayson, Landon, and Steve
(family time after Landon's game)**

Photographs

Signed to tour with Ball Up Streetball

JANELLE WEISS

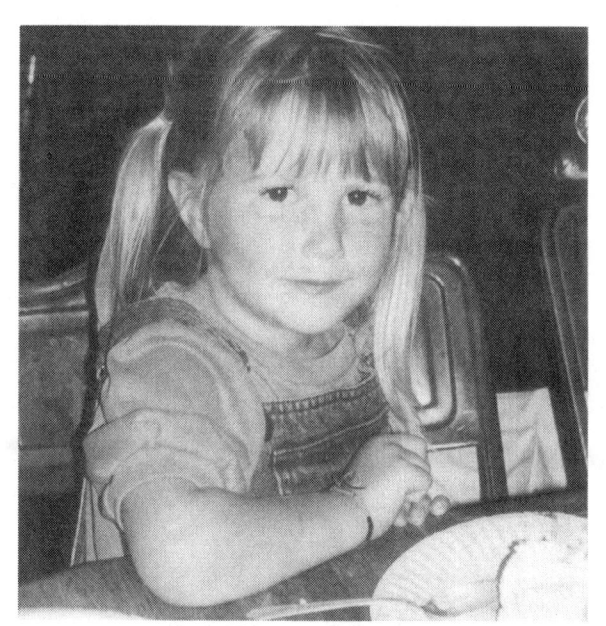

Janelle as a little girl

Janelle's senior year at West Salem High School

2008 – Eric and Janelle

Photographs

2008-2009 basketball season at Southridge High

July 2013 – Steven and Janelle

August 2012 before University of Idaho departure

Eric, Earleen, Steven, Janelle, and Paul

Photographs

ALEX HURLBURT

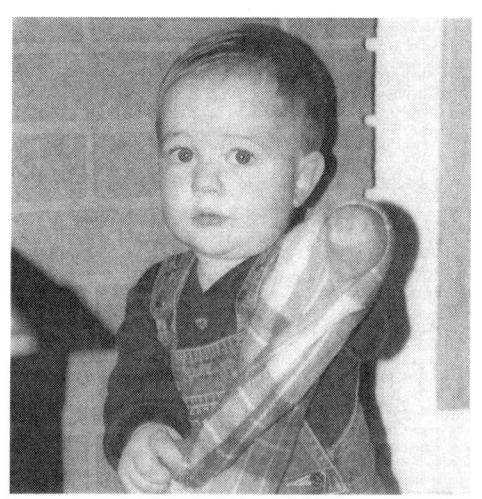

Alex as a toddler

Alex started playing baseball as a young boy

Sean and Alex

Boys and Girls Club football

Photographs

Playing basketball as a fifth grader

Boys and Girls Club basketball

Catcher for the West Salem JBO all-star team

Running bases

Photographs

Pitching for the all-star team

Julie, Alex, Ed, and Sean

AVRY HOLMES

The Holmes kids

**Teammate Kyle Atkinson and Avry
on an elite tourney team**

Photographs

His mom, Cathy, and Avry

His dad, Rick, and Avry

Adrian and Avry in a tournament in Salem, Oregon

Summer of 2012 before heading to the University of San Francisco

Photographs

BROOKE CHUHLANTSEFF

Brooke as a toddler

Brooke with her Awesome 3000 medal

Brooke made it to nationals in Jr. Olympics

Brooke, Madison, and Logan

Photographs

Brooke finds time to relax

Daniela, Madison, Brooke, Donald, and Logan

2013 – Cross-country teammates and Brooke

2013 – Way ahead of the pack at the district meet

Photographs

Brooke approaches finish line

**Brooke captures district championship
two years in a row**

Number one in the Central Valley Conference

DANIEL BRATTAIN

Freshman year at local sandwich place

Photographs

Hanging out in Keizer, Oregon

Daniel after competing in the 110 meter high hurdles in Jr. Olympics

Daniel takes the lead on a hurdle race

2013 – Senior picture

BRITTNEY KISER

Brittney as a baby

At Diamond Lake in Oregon

2012-2013 – freshman year swimming

Sunriver on the Deschutes River

Photographs

2013 – Bowling tournament champion

2013 – Gutting out a fish at Diamond Lake

At a swim meet

Jon, Scott, Tim, Tara, and Brittney

Photographs

NOAH TORRES

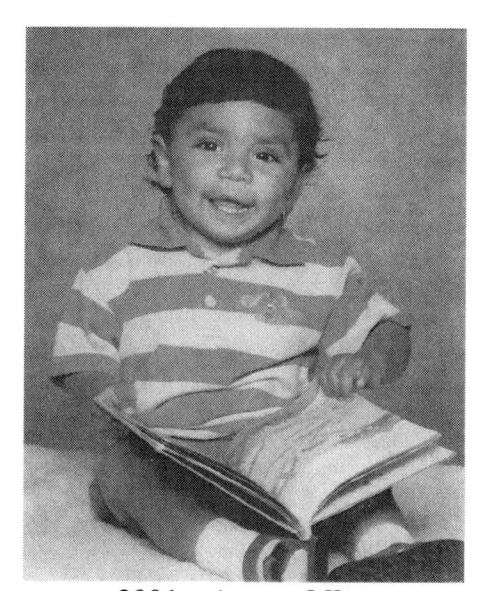

2001 – As a toddler

Moses Lake Soccer League

2002 – Tee ball

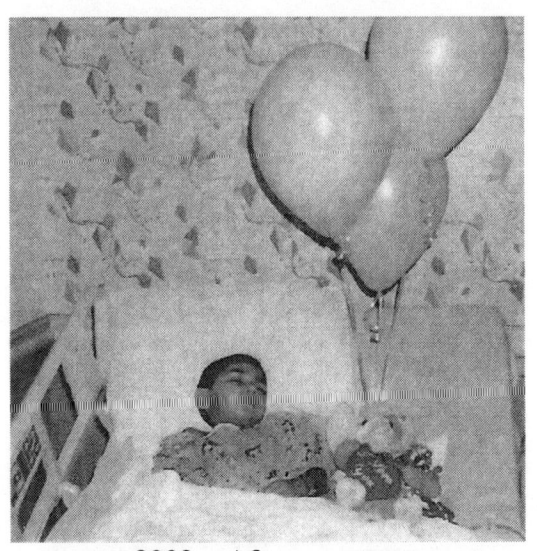

2002 – After surgery

Photographs

2004 – Building a snowman

2010 – Grade school days

2011 – Moses Lake All Stars

Audra, Angelica, Sophie, Paul, Noah, Paul Jr., and Amanda

The Avry Holmes Story
Like Father Like Son

Most high school basketball players dream of playing NCAA Division I Basketball. That dream is accomplished by very few athletes. Avry Holmes is one of those athletes that reached that dream, but it wasn't easy for the young man. Before his freshman year of basketball tryouts, a terrible tragedy hit his family hard.

Avry was born in Salem, Oregon, at Salem Hospital in 1994. He is the son of Rick and Cathy Holmes. His parents both played college basketball at Willamette University. They were both great college athletes and continued playing in city league games after college. Avry was born into a basketball family.

Rick was a manager and counselor for the Oregon Youth Authority at Hillcrest Correctional Facility. Cathy was a Business Analyst for the Department of Human Services. They both continued those careers. Cathy is a Latina and Rick is a Black man. Their family grew to six total kids. You can imagine their lives being very busy.

Avry has three older brothers, half-brother Ricky Jr., Austin, and Adrian. He's also blessed with two older sisters, half-sister Brandi, and Latrice. Avry is the youngest of the six kids.

"Avry is the baby of the family – he was always following his brothers and sisters and wanted to play basketball with them. In fact, anything they played he wanted to join in," Cathy said.

As he started growing it was evident that he had some natural talent in just about any sport he wanted to play. He was a great soccer player, a great baseball player, and a great football player. But the sport he fell in love with was basketball. He would follow his mom and dad around everywhere they went, especially if it had to do with basketball.

There was a basketball facility called The Hoop in Salem. Rick worked there as a referee for extra money. During the year there were several basketball leagues going on and tournaments of all kinds for youths, adults, college players, etc. Sometimes one job just isn't enough to feed a large family plus friends that come over regularly.

Cathy threw lingerie parties for extra money – I won't get into the details of that. Whatever they needed to do to support their family, they would do with honor and a great attitude. They didn't mind a full house of friends anytime of the day. Rick usually did the cooking in large batches.

"I remember watching Avry kick a soccer ball when he was a little kid. He would try and kick it but fell over several times. He was the type of kid that was going to get it right. He was focused and determined. After several attempts he finally kicked the ball and it flew a few yards," Cathy said.

Avry was amazing! As a four-year-old boy he would play soccer with first graders – on his sister Latrice's team. His dad coached soccer and didn't mind adding his son to the team. He would shine among the players. He was quick and coordinated. As a youngster, whatever sport he played he would always play two grades up. He was that much more advanced than his age-group athletes. Rick made sure that Avry had every opportunity to play any sport his older brothers or sisters played. He was a dad that made sure the youngest didn't get left out.

"The funny thing is that the older siblings would always blame Avry for everything. If they accidentally broke a lamp or something while playing, they would always set Avry up for the blame. And I found out about this when the kids were out of high school. How could we possibly get mad at Avry with his beautiful eyes and smile?" Cathy laughs.

Adrian and Austin often went to play basketball with their friends. They didn't really want Avry tagging along because he was still very little. To their knowledge he would hurt their team and they would lose.

One day Avry really wanted to go with his brothers to play basketball – he didn't want to miss an opportunity. Rick and Cathy stood by him and insisted that his brothers take him with them. So it was a done deal and Avry won the battle.

At the playground, Avry was playing on his brothers' team. The opponents thought of an easy victory over the Holmes brothers since they had little Avry playing. To make a long story short, Avry tore it up. He was driving to the hoop, shooting the ball outside, making steals, etc. This was an awakening to the opposing boys playing. They could not believe that a little kid could help defeat them.

Adrian and Austin started using their little brother as a secret weapon. Anyone they played assumed they would win because of little Avry playing – bad news for them, an awakening of assuming before knowing. Avry had made the brothers a better team.

Rick and Cathy always wanted the best for their kids. They wanted to put them in a position to succeed academically first. It was really important to them that they get an education.

"We wanted our kids to be smart. Academics were more important to us than sports. We knew how tough it was to make it in this world without an education. We got tired of hearing the phrase 'dumb jocks are a dime a dozen.' We didn't just want this for Avry, but for all of our kids as well. And since they would be playing sports, well, it was priority for them to have the grades before playing any sport. We wanted them to be intelligent young people. I was very blessed to have Ricky's support on this," Cathy said.

Rick taught his son so much about basketball and life in general. For Avry to have a dad as a best friend and to be around him all the time ... was priceless. Rick taught him how to work hard to earn respect – it was one of the first things. He would allow his son to go everywhere he went so he could learn from him. Playing one-on-one and teaching him valuable skills while playing the game was a treasure. Avry was never spoon-fed by his dad, he was taught to grind hard for what he got – he was raised to be a tough leader. Avry and his father were very close – a great father-son relationship.

Avry's mom was close to him as well. There were times when she had to do a workout at The Hoop – she'd take Avry with her. There were several ladies working out on the upstairs area of the facility. Cathy would encourage Avry to shoot baskets on the small hoops located upstairs. The moms could watch their kids while they exercised.

He never bought into that idea. He wanted to shoot baskets where the grownups shot baskets. That happened to be downstairs in the gym area where the rims were ten feet – the regulation height.

"When I was little I'd watch my mom and dad play basketball. Being around them in that environment inspired me to fall in love with the game. I started playing basketball every day," Avry said.

Avry attended Marion Miller Elementary School and Houck Middle School, both in Salem. His sister, Latrice, attended these schools with him.

"Avry was a happy kid that always had many friends. He was also a goof-ball type kid and liked to have fun – joking around with his friends. But at the same time he was the one they all came to for advice, if they were dealing with an issue. I guess he was like a counselor to them," Cathy said.

His mom speaks of how she always made sure that he had his homework done before going out to play. It was important to her and Rick. She helped him with anything he needed as far as school assignments. She wanted to make sure he learned what was being taught at the schools. It was also challenging taking kids to practices and then fixing dinner for everyone including friends that would come over to their house.

Avry learned well. On Mondays after school, the first thing he would want to do is finish his homework. His mom insisted on him taking a break, but he didn't want that. He wanted to get it done so he could go out and play basketball.

After basketball his friends would join him at the house for dinner or snacks. They would eat up a storm – the Holmes were a welcoming family to all of his friends.

"It was crazy at our house with all of our kids plus their friends. Ricky would cook up a large batch of waffles or whatever was on the menu to feed an army of kids at our house. But it was fun for all of us – we all just hung out and had a blast," Cathy said.

Avry stopped playing soccer in the fifth grade, but continued with football and baseball a few more years. He would focus on signing up to play basketball with a local AAU team called The Thunder Cats. The following year he played with the Wildcats sponsored by Dave Withnell and coached by Jerry Moore. He played the point guard position and contributed every time he set foot on the court.

During grade school he played one year of basketball in the Skyball League, which was a league of different schools competing against each other – then concluding with a Skyball League Tournament at the end of the season.

His eighth grade year he played for the Portland Hoop Kings, an AAU traveling team that played in competitive tournaments. This team was coached by Mike Plank, Sam Lapray, and Mike McShane (a former University of Oregon Duck). Mike Plank played at Willamette University – he introduced techniques and many aspects of the game. Mike also encouraged Avry to become a decent young man. He served as a mentor to Avry.

The Portland Hoop Kings started when Sam Lapray got together with Virgil Goss. Virgil was from Portland, Oregon, and had a son that also played AAU ball. They formed a team of talented athletes from the area. It was like an all-star team – a very well-balanced group. The team traveled to different cities and played in some of the biggest tournaments. We're talking about 6' 5" eighth graders that played in these tournaments. Some teams came from as far as New York – it was a huge deal and very competitive.

Avry became friends with this group of kids, AJ Lapray (recruited by University of Oregon to play basketball), Junior Espitia (recruited by University of Cal to play football), Justin Burgess (three-sport athlete at McNary and South High), Sam Lyon (football at North Salem High), Kyle Atkinson (recruited by Concordia University), Carson Hannibal (recruited by Pacific for football), Brenden Schaffer (West Salem sports), Nolan Hansen (recruited by Oregon State University), and Chase Cochran (recruited by Colorado State for football). All of these athletes were major contributors to the Portland Hoop Kings.

Some of the kids on the team were still learning and gaining confidence. Avry had that confidence from the get-go beginning of this team. Playing with his older brothers at a very young age instilled that hard confidence. He set an example for his teammates.

"My son, Sam, played with Avry during his middle school days. Avry is a great player. Every time he brought the ball down the court, teams never challenged him – the full-court press would go away. When they did press, not a problem, it was broken with his ball-handling skills and quickness. He is a quality person and a leader for any team he plays for. He was raised to be a fine young man – it truly shows," Jeremy Lyon said.

Avry seemed to be shining in tournaments capturing all-tournament awards and valuable experiences. He was playing with some of the best players in the state of Oregon and against some of the best players nationwide. Most importantly, he was sharing this with his entire family and friends – family was very important to him.

He started following his dad around everywhere he went. If Rick had a game to officiate, Avry was there. If Rick had a game to play in, Avry was there. Learning constantly from his dad and loving every minute of it. He just wanted to be around his dad and anything that had to do with basketball.

Avry had some close friends that he often hung around with during school or after school. They include, Jesus Ortiz, Guillermo Monroy, Josh Montero, Ben Shed, Jorge Rico, Divine Jacobo, and Queen Dash. They were his closest friends of the many that came to his house. There were times where eight or nine kids came over to eat or just hang out. They would do homework together and support one another in whatever they faced.

"I remember one time the boys were hanging out late at the house. They ended up sleeping on the living room floor. The next morning, Ricky fixed his specialty – a large batch of hash browns with bacon. They downed a lot of food. It was always like that around our house. We always had kids over and big feasts," Cathy said.

Entering his freshman year at North Salem High School, Avry was so excited for the basketball season to start. He was pumped that his dad was going to get that chance to see him play basketball in high school. They did everything together – like father like son. But first, his dad would get to watch him play football. Avry played just about every position.

He enjoyed being the defensive end – that gave him the chance to sack the quarterback. He also played wide receiver and quarterback. A great athlete on the football field as well.

When football season was over the anticipation for the start of an amazing basketball career couldn't have been any sweeter. Avry was excited about the coming tryouts for the varsity basketball team. His mom and dad were very proud of him and looking forward to watching him play high school basketball – a dream for the entire family.

The daily-morning routine for the Holmes was pretty normal I would say. Cathy would be the first one up to get ready for work. She'd leave early and would not see the kids in the morning. Rick would start his morning by yelling at the kids every five minutes.

"Avry, time to get up – come on time for school! Latrice, you too ... let's go, get up!" Rick yelled.

Rick's voice motivated them to wake up and get ready for school. This happened every school morning. He would cook breakfast for them and send them off before leaving for work himself. He was a devoted father and loved his children passionately – wanted the very best for them. He took good care of his family. We need more fathers in this world like Rick Holmes.

On Monday, November 3, 2008, a life-changing experience was about to happen to the entire family. There was not a voice yelling at the kids in the morning. Latrice eventually woke up and noticed it was almost time for school. She went to knock on Avry's bedroom door and yelled at him to wake up – it was time for school. She was a little puzzled because for the first time her dad didn't wake them up. The two kids rushed to get ready and then left for school. Latrice did feel that it was a very unusual morning.

Cathy and Rick were very close and always called each other to communicate. Cathy had not heard from Rick all morning and decided to call him – she wanted to make sure the kids made it to school. The phone rang and rang, but there was no answer.

"It was about 9:30 a.m. Ricky always answered if I called in the mornings – I found this to be out of the norm. I decided to take a break from work to see what was up with Ricky," Cathy said.

When Cathy arrived at her home, she noticed that Rick's car was still parked on the driveway. She walked in the house yelling for him but there was no answer. The house was very quiet, maybe a few things laying around on the table and the bedroom doors all open.

"I went into the bathroom to see if he was there, because normally he would spend a long time in there getting ready. Ricky! No sign of him there, I continued to walk to our bedroom," Cathy said.

When Cathy walked into the bedroom, she saw Rick lying on the floor next to the bed with one of his arms reaching for the phone – he must have been like that for a long while. He was looking at her, but could not talk. It was like he made every effort to call 911, but just could not reach the phone.

Cathy called 911 immediately. The ambulance paramedics rushed over and showed up at their house. For Cathy to see her husband on a stretcher was a shock – her breath was taken, heart downed, and eyes wide open. They took him to Salem Hospital.

Latrice, Adrian, Austin, and Brandi drove to North Salem High School to pick up Avry before heading to Salem Hospital. It hit Avry hard – he was clinging to his sister and brothers. At the hospital they were all concerned and in a huge state of shock.

This couldn't be happening to the father that was very active and full of joy around his family. The whole world changed to this close family in a blink of an eye.

This precious dad was then put on a life flight to OHSU (Oregon Health Science University) in Portland, Oregon – a university of medicine, nursing, dentistry, and research. This hospital specializes in a wide range of personal injuries, illnesses and diseases. Rick had suffered a hypertensive intracerebral hemorrhage – a type of stroke which causes bleeding to the brain.

"When I found out that Ricky was going to be put on a life flight to Portland, I thought to myself, how ironic because he was always afraid of flying," Cathy said.

The family drove up to Portland and remained there for a couple of days praying and waiting for any positive thing that could come about.

Avry had his head resting on his father's chest. He was in tears telling his dad that from now on he was doing everything for him. He promised him the world. Avry promised his dad that he was going to make him proud.

Later that evening some of the kids drove back home to get cleaned up – plus take care of some errands. Cathy and Adrian stayed in Portland the entire time.

Brandi, Austin, and Latrice could not sleep all night. Avry was torn emotionally and could not stop thinking about his dad – tears running down his face. At 2:00 a.m. Adrian's picture popped up on Latrice's caller ID. She had an idea that it was not good news. Adrian let them know that they needed to come say goodbye because Dad wasn't going to make it. Rick Holmes passed away later that morning.

He was a nurturing father to his family. He was full of life and stressed to his kids that he wanted them to be successful individuals that worked hard to earn their rewards.

Latrice couldn't stop thinking of how her dad would not be there for special events. She kept thinking of graduations, birthdays, weddings, grandkids. Rick would not be there to share precious moments, but he would be there in spirit and in her heart.

This changed Latrice as a person. She used to think about herself a lot. She now thinks about being closer to her little brother, Avry, who had grown to be a young man. She thinks about all the things her dad did for her and cherishes all of those moments. Latrice realized how important family was and not to take it for granted.

The Holmes kids had a rough time dealing with the tragedy. In one second everything can change – life is so precious. They were blessed to have had a dad that shared many things with them. Avry found strength within to carry on with his plans. The plans his dad supported and encouraged all the days he spent with him. He wanted to play NCAA Division I Basketball someday. With his dad now gone, it was going to be an obstacle to overcome and prevail with his dream. This young man took what happened and turned it into something positive. He was going to make his dad proud in everything he did – no matter how hard he had to work.

His mom, Cathy, was torn and hurt bad – she had lost her partner in life. She was a strong lady and fought through to make the necessary adjustments.

"I feel that Ricky is still here. Avry promised his dad he would take care of me. I don't doubt that a bit. Avry has a big heart, I remember one time I had just played in a city league game in Eugene. I hurt my ankle really bad. The next day I was lying on the couch resting, Avry had made a computer-generated card that read, '*Mom, I'm sorry you got hurt in the game. Get well soon – I love you.*' That really touched me that he would care enough to do that," Cathy said.

Friends are so important to have for support. At that time Avry had a girlfriend who was a track star. Alyssa Neal was there to support him and stand by him. Queen Dash was his best friend and always there to talk if he needed. Avry would often talk about things with her – like counseling. Queen played basketball for the women's team at McKay High School. Queen would often bring Avry candy if he was injured or struggling with something.

After days had gone by and things were starting to settle a little, it was getting close to basketball tryouts at North Salem High School. Coach Joseph Cho, who was the head varsity basketball coach, talked to Cathy and informed her that Avry did not need to be at tryouts. He understood what he had gone through. That evening Cathy talked to Avry about what Coach Cho said.

"Avry looked at me and said, 'I'm not having that, I'm gonna be there.' Nothing was going to stop him from being at the tryouts. He knew his dad would want that. Ricky taught him to be tough and to work hard for what he earned. It was like he was hearing Ricky talk," Cathy said.

Avry was ready for basketball tryouts after school. Preparing to go out onto the basketball court, he was feeling very nervous. He threw up – his stomach was in knots. He cleaned up and headed toward the gym. The players all felt bad for Avry and sympathized with him. But they were all fighting for a spot on the team and were not going to make anything easy for him.

Avry worked hard, making shots, playing defense, and running all kinds of drills. It was like a kid with a focused mind to accomplish anything that came his way. Basketball helped Avry deal with the loss of his dad. He became more driven on the basketball court.

By the end of the week the basketball tryouts had come to an end. The coaches had to make all of the cuts and determine what players would make up the freshman team, junior varsity team, and varsity team. Avry was selected to play on the varsity team as a freshman – he became a North Salem Viking.

"We were all so proud of him. He had worked so hard through the years for this moment. We all had Ricky in our thoughts. We shared this moment with him – he's up there," Cathy said.

North Salem was a rebuilding team at the time. They weren't at the top of the CVC League (Central Valley Conference), but with Avry coming into the program things would progress throughout his high school career.

Before entering high school, he had friends and coaches try to influence him to attend their school. It was mostly with the AAU players he developed friendships with. The whole idea was to create a powerhouse team that could compete at the state level. Avry never bought into that. He wanted to stay grounded on the north side of Salem – his neighborhood. If someone wanted to play with him, they would have to join him at North Salem High School.

Playing time during his freshman year was great. He was getting a lot of minutes as a freshman and contributing at the varsity level. He was a type of player that respected the seniors and did not want to step on any toes. He was careful with his shot selection and mostly focused on distributing the ball. He still managed to score points but not as many as he could have.

He developed a great player/coach relationship with Coach Cho. The North Salem Vikings started improving every year. The second year Avry was taking the lead role as the starting point guard. This made the Vikings a more solid team. To have a point guard like Avry Holmes would be any coach's dream.

At the end of Avry's sophomore year, Coach Cho made a decision to retire from coaching for family reasons. This coach was like a father to Avry – he was a mentor and friend. Once again it was sad that he was going to lose someone else in his life.

It was a rough situation for this young man. He struggled for a while and just fought through hard times. Sometimes it's difficult to understand why things happen to good people.

Avry would often go to The Hoop (a basketball facility) to practice and play pickup games. One day he met Willie Freeman. Willie played professional basketball overseas for a few years with teams in countries like, Argentina, Luxembourg, and a few others.

"I had just got done working out that day – waiting for my agent to call me. I was playing competitively at the time. I noticed a young kid shooting baskets and working on some moves. I watched and noticed that his shooting form was not quite right. So I introduced myself and showed him a few things. He picked them up really fast," Willie said.

Avry got to know Willie and really liked him as an individual. Willie started showing this young man how to shoot his 3-ball with more accuracy. He also helped him with ball-handling and all sorts of skills.

Avry was very particular on whom he learned from and Willie seemed to really fit the mold on just about everything. Willie would train at The Hoop and then work with Avry several times.

With Coach Cho now gone, the North Salem Vikings would need a new coach. Avry really liked Willie and was going to do whatever he could to bring him to North Salem.

The only experience Willie had as a coach was at Western Carolina University, where he played college basketball with Kevin Martin. Kevin, at the time, played with the Oklahoma City Thunder. Avry got to meet Kevin when he came down to Salem to visit Willie. That was an amazing experience for him. To talk and play with an NBA player would be any kid's dream. Avry had that opportunity, plus, he learned even more about the game from Kevin and Willie.

"I think the world of Avry Holmes – he's the one that vouched for me to become the head coach at North Salem High School. Avry is a hard-nosed player that studies the game well. He wants to be the best he can be. There aren't too many kids that work as hard as Avry these days," Willie said.

    Willie was eventually hired to be the head coach at North Salem. He was a young Black man that knew the game well and could relate with the players very well. The North Salem area is a very diverse area – Willie was great for the program. That gave Avry hope for a great season. Willie was like a big brother to him and an inspiration.

    During one of the regular season games, Willie was the head coach, and North Salem was playing McNary at North. Head Coach Matt Espinoza was rebuilding a team of young players at McNary. This was the second meeting of the year. North dominated the McNary Celtics the first meeting of the season. So naturally they were feeling a little overconfident before this game.

    Avry was distributing the ball in the first half. He was one that always tried to get his team involved. McNary had improved tremendously from the previous meeting. All of a sudden North was struggling with McNary's defense. The traps were causing the Vikings to turn the ball over and the defensive pressure was causing them to miss shot after shot.

The North Salem Vikings found themselves down – trailing by fifteen at the half. Could this be happening? The number one team in the CVC was trailing to the number five team.

The second half, Avry stepped it up a notch, L.J. Westbrook started making steals, and Shai Gray was a rebounding monster. The rest of the team followed Avry's lead. Everyone could see how focused and determined Avry was – he was not about to lose this game. The difference in the game was the three-point shooting by Avry that helped the Vikings prevail by a few points at the end of the game. They had come back from a fifteen-point deficit. The Celtics were in disbelief of what had just happened. The inexperience of the young Celtic squad showed in the second half.

The North Salem Vikings became the 2010 CVC League Champions. Avry Holmes was one of the reasons this team was so successful. The entire North Salem team was supportive of his style of play. He utilized all of his strengths.

"Yes sir, Avry is special, but to this day I feel that every young man on that team played a role and contributed to our success. The seniors that worked hard at practice to make us better, to the talent around Avry that worked together," Willie said.

Coach Freeman and Avry became very close. Willie was a mentor and friend and enjoyed being around Avry. He remembers something that happened while he was on a date one evening.

"I was having fun being on a date. It was about 9:00 p.m. or so. Avry calls me up," Willie said.

"Hey coach, I need to go shoot at the gym ... where you at?"

"I'm on a date Avry – not gonna happen tonight," Willie hangs up.

Phone rings again, "Coach, come on man, I need the keys to the gym I want to shoot some hoops. I need to practice."

"Avry, I'm on a date don't you understand that?"

"A date! That's not important, come on man I need the keys to shoot some buckets."

That's how it went sometimes with Willie and Avry. Avry was that close to Willie that he could rely on him even when he was on a date.

"Willie Freeman was an inspiration to me. He helped me with so much. My three-point shooting improved tremendously after he had worked with me. I think he is a great person and I have a lot of respect for him," Avry said.

While Willie helped Avry with many things, Avry put some time in himself. He watched other point guards (whether NBA or college) that might fit his style of play. He studied them and soaked in the details of their moves and creations. He worked on dribbling skills, defensive skills. He even started a jump program to improve his leaping abilities. In a matter of time, he started dunking the ball easily.

"One of my favorite basketball moments with Avry had to be at Marshfield High School in Coos Bay, Oregon. It was the Les Schwab Holiday Tournament. We were playing North Bend and one of our players, Ricky Johal, had just grabbed the rebound. Ricky started dribbling down court and saw Avry ahead. He passed it to him. Avry must have taken one dribble and then dunked on number 14 – who fell back on his butt. Avry just looked at him and walked away," Willie said.

After the season was over, Avry joined The Northwest Panthers, a team from Bellevue, Washington, that was coached by Gary Ward. Bellevue is roughly a four-hour drive from Salem, Oregon. The Panthers were an AAU elite team that had a top-notch roster. Avry would play with some of the best players in the northwest. This would be an opportunity for him to play in huge tournaments against prep schools. Some teams were from New York, Los Angeles, etc. There was only one problem, the team practiced every other weekend in Bellevue and the tournaments would be all summer long.

Cathy and Avry worked out a plan for him. He would take the Greyhound Bus to Portland. From there he would pick up the Amtrak to Bellevue, Washington.

This was a high school kid who had lost his father and was by himself now. Most kids would probably be scared and not ready for an adventure like this at such a young age. Not Avry, he was a tough kid.

"I was so excited to meet my teammates and to be part of a great team like this. I wasn't scared at all. I enjoy traveling by myself and just being away on my own for the first time," Avry said.

He would stay overnight at the coach's house or some of his teammates' houses before returning to Salem. It was a great experience that he cherished and will remember for a long time to come.

"My coach was very accommodating. One time the train was not operating due to some bad weather. It was raining really hard and there might have been some kind of mudslide. They were afraid the train could slip off the rail. My coach drove me all the way back to Salem that night," Avry said.

Avry was a pretty strong kid at 6' 1" and muscle definition – he could handle himself. One time he was riding on the train and he met a person from Louisiana. This person was drunk and was saying a lot of funny things. Avry was keeping an eye on him, but at the same time he thought this guy was cool. Traveling on Amtrak or Greyhound bus you meet many strange but interesting people. You always have to watch for yourself – you never know the people well enough to have that trust.

The summer came to an end and Avry gained valuable experience playing with solid players from the northwest, and being out on his own away from home.

His senior year, 2011, there were several Division I colleges very interested in him – some as early as his junior year. The North Salem Vikings were playing against Corvallis, Oregon, at the Central Catholic Tournament. This game was really important because recruiters from a major college were there scouting Avry.

Several Colleges were interested, Washington State, University of Washington, UCLA, University of San Francisco, and a few others. But the college recruiters that were at this tournament happened to be from Georgia Tech. They were excited to see this young man play and to hopefully join their squad next year.

During the game, Avry went down with a lot of pain to his right knee. The entire North Salem bench was in a silent mode and concerned. Georgia Tech held their breath for a bit. Avry faced yet another obstacle. After what he had endured previously, this must have shattered his heart. The result after an MRI was a torn meniscus to his right knee.

"This was heartbreaking for Avry. He had waited a long time to play at the Les Schwab Tournament at the Rose Garden in Portland. And the tournament was coming up soon," Cathy said.

Avry and his family had some decisions to make as far as surgery. Could he play with a tear on his knee the rest of the season? They knew his future was in jeopardy and if he was going to play college ball, it had to be done the right way.

Arthroscopic knee surgery was performed on Avry's right knee. It was successful, but he would have to sit out a few weeks while he recovered. He started therapy and worked hard to build up the muscles that supported his knee. It seemed like eternity to him – waiting for the knee to heal and his full strength to come back.

Meanwhile his team continued playing. They lost a few games because of Avry's absence, but they won a few as well. His team held the ground just enough for their starting point guard to return. The entire team wore shooting shirts that read "Believe" on them.

Holmes recovered eventually from knee surgery. He worked through the pain and returned to action toward the end of the season with a few games remaining. His first game back they were facing a very good team. The Sprague Olympians were one of the top teams in the CVC, and his former teammate from AAU basketball, AJ Lapray, played for them.

Avry was not 100 percent but he managed to play well in this game. They came up short losing to Sprague, but won the rest of the games after that. He kept improving every game he played. His knee was sore and ice was a necessity after every game.

The North Salem Vikings went on to win the CVC title once again. The celebrations would start and Avry Holmes had helped North Salem win back-to-back CVC titles.

While everyone from North was hoping to head to the 6A OSAA State Tournament in Portland, Oregon, they had to get by one playoff game. They would have to travel to South Medford.

The following week they would get on the bus and head south on I-5. After a four-hour drive they arrived at South Medford. Entering the gym that evening, they wore their warm-up shirts that read "Believe" – they were pumped and ready to go. Unfortunately, being the visiting team in a hostile environment could mean the team might be playing against five players plus the officials.

"Avry never gets a technical foul called on him. He was one of the captains on the team and was asking the official for an explanation of a questionable call he made. He got Td up – a technical foul. Normally I don't blame officials for a game we lose. But at South Medford the officials were terrible. Our team consisted of a lot of Black kids and Hispanic kids. South Medford had mostly White kids. I felt that the officials were favoring South Medford heavily. I didn't think it was fair. But there was nothing we could do about it. Avry's dream of playing in the state tournament came to an end. I was very sad and thought North Salem could have represented better at the tournament," Cathy said.

Rick and Cathy always taught their kids that they would run into situations where there might be a little discrimination based on their color. Sadly it's real ... even today. They experienced discrimination mostly at away tournaments when the kids were younger.

"Ricky and I told our kids that they had to overlook those kinds of things. They had to be tough and ignore people like that. If they were going to be successful in anything, they had to realize that some people are just ignorant. We would tell them to stay strong and avoid that distraction. I think Avry did that, even during the South Medford game," Cathy said.

Avry was selected to be the 2012 Central Valley Conference Player of the Year. He also received first team all-state honors. In his senior year, this 6' 1" point guard averaged 20.9 points, 6.3 assists, 4.8 rebounds, and 3.3 steals. He lead his team to two consecutive CVC titles his junior and senior years. And to go along with a successful high school basketball career, he maintained a 3.4 GPA – perfect start for a college career.

Basketball has taught Avry Holmes so much. He has a passion for the game and every time he steps on that basketball court he plays for his dad.

"Basketball has taught me discipline. My teammates look up to me. I want to do the right things, not only on the court, but off the court as well. Basketball has taught me to get socially involved, because in life you need that. My parents always taught me to do the right things. No one's perfect, sometimes you make mistakes, but being part of a basketball team you learn from experiences – carrying that the rest of your life. Basketball has been a priority for me, it's taught me so many things," Avry said.

It was time for Avry to make a decision of what college he was going to attend. Boston College, Cal-Poly, Harvard, U of O, OSU, etc. Several schools were interested.

Time after time through the season, there he was sitting on the bleachers, Assistant Coach Michael Lee. He was a former Kansas Jayhawk, but now coaching at the University of San Francisco. Michael would drive ten hours to watch Avry play basketball. He kept showing up at games throughout the year. He would talk to Avry after the games showing strong interest. Rex Walters was the head coach at San Francisco. Rex played in the NBA for ten years from 1993 to 2003. He played for the New Jersey Nets, the Philadelphia 76ers, and the Miami Heat.

"Coach Rex Walters is a winning coach and highly respected. They let me know that I would be playing the 2 position – I would be contributing to the team right away. I really felt that playing for Rex Walters would give me the opportunity to play in front of NBA scouts," Avry said.

In the spring of 2012, Avry Holmes signed to play Division I Basketball with the University of San Francisco. He became a Don. He was headed to the bay area, the city is well known by the Golden Gate Bridge, Alcatraz Island, and Chinatown. These are just a few of the many tourist attractions the city has to offer. It is a city worth traveling to visit. And maybe even to catch one of the Don's games.

"When I think of Avry Holmes I think of 'overcome.' He overcame so many obstacles during his young life. A serious ankle injury, fighting through the knee surgery, and losing his dad before his freshman year of basketball," Willie Freeman said.

Avry wears number 12 on his game jersey. The "1" stands for his father and the "2" stands for him – like father like son. He also has a tattoo across his chest that reads, "Like father like son." His dad is always in his heart.
I saw the University of San Francisco Dons play against 6' 10" Dwight Powell and the Standford Cardinal. As a freshman, Avry scored 17 points in 25 minutes. A start of a fine career in college – he knocked down threes from each side of the basket.

Avry's mom, Cathy, wants to give parents some advice. She encourages every parent to stay positive and support what your kids want to do.

"Let them know that it's attainable. Ask them what their plan is and what they need to do to get there. If they know you have their back, they'll feel more confident. I'm so proud of Avry. The hard work he put in has paid off for him. Ricky is up there and I feel like I can hear him saying how proud he is of Avry," Cathy said.

In his first year of playing college basketball he was named to the All-Freshman Team in the WAC Conference. He has big plans for the future.

"I would really love to play in the NBA someday – I believe that it can happen. If I ever get to the point where I make a lot of money, I would be sure to give back to the community. If that doesn't work out, I would love to have a job that helps kids. I enjoy being around kids and teaching them positive things. My dad had a job that helped troubled kids – it would be an honor to follow in his footsteps," Avry said.

Avry Holmes is truly grateful to have a mom like Cathy. He speaks very highly of her and feels very blessed to have had her love and support. He doesn't know what he would have done without her.

"Mom gave me rides to the games or wherever I needed to go. I tried not to ask her for too much help with my homework because I knew how hard she worked at her job. She was always there for me and took good care of me. She always made sure I was on the right track – she kept me away from negative influences. I love my mom and my family, I think family is really important," Avry said.

The sky's the limit for this young man who is focused on accomplishment. With his dad in his heart and his family next to him, he has a very bright future. Well done young man, you deserve all you have earned. Who knows, maybe in the future we'll see Avry in the NBA.

Brooke Chuhlantseff Has Olympic Trials Vision

It amazes me to see a young-female athlete compete with older athletes, and how she holds her own ground despite the age and physical development differences. To be a freshman in high school and to become a district champion among sophomores, juniors, and seniors, well, I think that says it all.

Brooke Chuhlantseff was born in Salem, Oregon, at Salem Hospital in 1998. She is the daughter of Donald and Daniela. Brooke has a brother, Logan, and a sister, Madison.

Donald played football (nose guard) for a junior college in Fresno, California. After that, he went on to play on an athletic scholarship at Arizona State University. He is now a motorcycle police officer. Daniela attended college at Arizona State University. She was a track and field athlete and specialized in the 3200 meters (now it's called the 3000 meters). She is now a fifth-grade teacher.

Brooke definitely takes after her parents in the sports world. She is a very intelligent blue-eyed blonde and has always had a personality that was on the shy side.

"She's a sweet girl and very nice to kids. Some kids think that just because she doesn't acknowledge them, she must be rude or stuck-up. But really, she's just a little shy," Daniela said.

Brooke was raised in a middle-income-class family and a normal neighborhood that often had kids around to play with. One of her best friends was Sarah Litwin.

"I've known Sarah for ten years. We've been through everything together. I could always count on her for any kind of support and to simply talk about anything," Brooke said.

When Brooke was a little girl in grade school, she never had any worries. Her neighborhood was fun and there was always an elementary group of kids to hang out with.
Brooke attended Brush College Elementary. Her PE teacher, Loni Espinoza, thinks very highly of her.

"Brooke is so focused at accomplishment. She is the total package. She has a great attitude, she's a hard worker, performs well academically, and is a strong athlete. Brooke is all of that while being very humble. This young lady also currently holds the fifth grade school record for the girls' mile run at 6:45.00 for Brush College Elementary," Mrs. Espinoza said.

In elementary school the homework was never an issue. Brooke was an outstanding student with top marks. She was a sweet little girl, but very competitive. If she was going to do something, it got done – very determined.

"Fifth grade was my best class ever. Outdoor school was special – no one cared about anything we just had fun," Brooke said.

In the earlier years, Donald and Daniela had no specific goals for any of their kids. They surely introduced many sports to them hoping there would be an interest.

"I signed Brooke up for tennis, basketball, and swimming. I just wanted her to be active in something," Daniela said.

Brooke seemed to take an interest in swimming. She began swimming and did very well at this sport – maybe something she could have taken seriously.

When Brooke was a toddler, her mom would push her in a jogging stroller as she ran around the neighborhood. When the toddler became a sixth grader, her mom would take her on short runs through the neighborhood. Mom and daughter would jog together – such a nice thing to see. At that age her mom took her running once a week.

Brooke would watch her mom as she ran alongside of her. How she paced herself, her breathing pattern, and how much fun she had. What a great workout it was when they returned home – a completed run. It was relaxing and motivating to Brooke knowing she had accomplished what her mom did.

"My mom let me run with her – she encouraged me to work at improving every day. I wanted to be like my mom. She inspired me to find a love for running," Brooke said.

At Brush College Elementary, Brooke made the Jaycee Relay Teams every year she tried out during her grade-school days. The relays at the time were sponsored by the Jaycee organization. This annual event was huge in the Salem/Keizer area. Most of the elementary schools participated in this community program that took place on a Saturday.

The four fastest runners would represent their school in a 4 x 100 meter relay – this was an all-day event. In addition, there was a 4 x 400 meter relay that was called the Mayor's Mile. In this event the top eight schools would compete in only one race, and again, the teams would consist of the fastest four kids of each school.

Chuhlantseff made both teams for her school and did very well. In the Mayor's Mile, her team placed third out of eight schools racing. Brooke ran a 1:10 split, Anna Norrenberns ran a 1:16 split, Loryn Erdrich ran a 1:21 split, and Amanda Robertson ran a 1:23 split. The best part is that Sarah Litwin, her best friend, was an alternate for the race. Brooke's time of 1:10 is the third best since 1996.

Brooke shined in all the races she ran. The event was held at Willamette University. This college has a large stadium-seating field that was packed every year for this event.

Another event she ran while in grade school was the Awesome 3000. This was a fund-raising event for the Salem-Keizer Education Foundation. This running event usually had around 3000 kids participating every year.

A heart-touching moment that her mom speaks about is something we can all learn from. When the race for Brooke's age group started, she was going strong and competing very well with the running crowd. She turned her head and noticed her friend, Sarah Hughes, falling behind and struggling to keep up with the crowd.

Everyone else seemed to be keeping the pace and moving faster. Brooke had a decision to make in a split second. She could have done very well in this race, but her heart told her to slow down and run with Sarah. She felt bad for Sarah and did not want her to fall behind all alone. She ran with Sarah and finished the race at the end of the pack. Brooke felt better knowing her friend was not alone at the end of the race – that was more important to her.

After participating in these running events, and knowing that she could possibly win, she gained a ton of confidence. She realized she could find success in competing in track and field.

By the time Brooke was promoted to sixth grade she was attending Walker Middle School and her mom was taking her running twice a week. After two years at Walker Middle School, she attended a new middle school that had just been built. Her eighth grade year was spent at Straub Middle School in West Salem. There weren't too many changes in the transition from grade school to middle school. But according to Brooke, one of the changes was constant homework.

When Brooke was in the seventh grade she was named to the All-City Salem/Keizer Track Team for setting first-place marks. In the 800 Meter Run she set a mark of 2:28 and in the 1500 Meter Run she won with a time of 5:08. This was the highest honor for a runner in the district.

During her middle school days Brooke was starting to get acknowledged for her gift in running. Her signature was "The Runner." Kids knew her as an athlete that was determined to win a race.

"My parents were so supportive of me, especially my mom. She was a runner and understood what I was experiencing or about to experience. It was always easy talking to her. When things were bad, she was always there to encourage me – she would find a way to lift me up," Brooke said.

One of the obstacles this young girl faced was deciding what sport to focus on. She was very good at swimming and enjoyed being part of a swimming team. Her heart kept telling her that running was going to be her sport.

"In middle school, I felt Brooke could do two sports, but in high school she would have to decide what sport to focus on. It was up to Brooke to decide what she wanted to do – which sport would possibly give her a college scholarship? I told Brooke she should try giving running a shot. She was winning races in just about every meet she competed in," Daniela expressed.

Daniela enrolled her daughter to compete in the Jr. Olympics. She would compete in the Youth Division. She did not belong to a track club, but that was okay because she could compete as Unattached. There are many advantages of belonging to a track club – however, if an athlete cannot commit to some of the requirements, they can choose to run as Unattached. It worked out for the Chuhlantseffs.

After her eighth-grade year, Brooke captured the state title in the 1500 meter run for the Youth Division. She advanced to the Jr. Olympic Regional Meet and won the silver medal. This advanced her to the National Jr. Olympic Meet in Baltimore, Maryland, at Morgan State University. She place 6th at nationals in 1500 meter run with a time of 4:51.84.

"My parents flew me to Baltimore and gave me the opportunity to run against the best youth girls in the nation. I couldn't have been more thankful for their support," Brooke said.

One of the most memorable awards Brooke received as a middle-school student was the Athlete of the Year Award for Straub Middle School. To win that award with so many kids competing was a huge accomplishment. I mean, we're talking about the entire school with a huge enrollment.

Brooke had challenges she had to face just because of her personality. People getting to know her had difficulties because she was very shy and didn't feel comfortable conversing with just anyone. This gave some of the students an impression that she might be stuck up or rude, but really she was more private and not as open as most kids.

"Brooke struggled with decision making as far as what sport to pursue in the future – what would she be most successful at? She hadn't experienced having a real coach. I was her coach to this point," Daniela said.

Brooke was the type of kid that had a few friends – no boyfriends. She would come home after school and immediately hit the books – her homework came first. Her grades included nothing but straight As. She was a very sharp student. This young lady was blessed with a gift of being able to retain knowledge. It just came easy to her. She is what you call a perfectionist – everything had to be perfect.

"I remember a time when she had a bulky snowsuit on. I was at the top of the steps in our house. Brooke slid all the way down the steps and landed on the floor. The look on her face when she turned her head and looked up at me, was priceless," Daniela said laughing.

Brooke's passion away from running and swimming is animals. Her parents would often take her to the Portland Zoo. She always wanted to somehow help the zoo staff. Penguins were one of her favorites.

"I love animals, I can certainly see myself someday working in a field that includes animals," Brooke said.

In the year 2012 Brooke was ready to enter high school. West Salem High School, in Salem Oregon, was acquiring a special young lady with athleticism. She was a dedicated student that would challenge herself in signing up for the toughest classes in school. She had a vision of college in the future. Her schedule would include honors classes such as, English, History, Math, and French.

She would receive college credit for the completion of these classes. In the academic department she was all set maintaining a 4.0 GPA in all of her honors classes – Brooke was a very intelligent cute blue-eyed blonde who defied the stereotype.

There was a time that she missed a science lab assignment. She wasn't too happy about that. The next day she asked the science teacher, Mr. Lambert, if she could make it up somehow. He was more than glad to accommodate. He assigned her a difficult project which consisted of writing up a challenging procedure to a science task. Her teacher's expression was very positive – he was very impressed. She wanted to maintain a 4.0 GPA and was about to do whatever it took.

Along with her seriousness and perfectionist attitude she managed to find time to be goofy. She would act silly and do off-the-wall things that were funny. It's always a good idea to have a little fun – I believe it helps keep the stress level balanced.

It was time for Brooke to focus on running. Her cross country meets were exciting to watch. Running against seniors and juniors and beating them at the district level was eye opening, basically because she was only a freshman. People would forget that she was not as developed but could hold her own ground.

At the end of the cross country season she found herself capturing the district title in the Central Valley Conference at Bush's Pasture Park with a time of 18:22. The conference consisted of six 6A schools, McNary; McKay; West Salem; Sprague; South Salem and North Salem. Brooke had won as a freshman – a huge accomplishment. Her season best of 18:15 in the 5000 meters was set at the Saxon XC Invitational Meet on September15th, 2012. She went on to place ninth in the Oregon State Cross Country Meet.

At the end of the season Brooke was named the All-Mid-Valley Athlete of the Year for cross country. As a freshman not too many kids get to experience such a prestigious award. Brooke is a special young lady that has dreams of running in the Olympic Trials someday – that's where she has set her standard for now.

"I know I'm young and chances of making it to the Olympics are a long stretch, so I'm going to be more realistic and set my goal for the Olympic Trials," Brooke smiles.

Competing in high school as a long distance runner would be a tougher challenge than in middle school. Not only the competition itself, but also because she loved swimming and was fairly good at it. Brooke was a member of a swim team called the Northwest Aquatics. She trained with her team at the South Salem Tennis/Swim Club.

Brooke would struggle with her own mind and sometimes even get depressed. Which sport would she choose to focus on for college? She was competing in cross country races in the fall – excelling at the cross country running events, and competing in swim meets in the winter. Swimming was fun for her, she loved being around her friends, Gabby Haugen and Maddie Blissit.

She helped her swim team capture the district championship and they advanced to the state championship meet.

"I like being around my friends that do sports, it's so easy to relate to them because they go through the same things I do," Brooke said.

As the winter season started coming to an end, Brooke started realizing that as much as she enjoyed swimming, she was leaning toward cross country and track and field. She would have to stop swimming competitively to improve her times in her running events. She decided that running was going to be the best choice for her.

"Being a freshman I hadn't really experienced too much of high school. I made a few friends but it was also difficult to talk to certain kids – I was a little shy I guess. High school is supposed to be a memorable adventure. Those are the years you remember for a long time. As far as sports in high school, I've made up my mind that I will take running more serious from now on," Brooke said.

When a decision like that is made, it becomes easier for the athlete to focus on the sport they want to excel in. Brooke had less stress in her mind – she felt more relieved that she had a driven direction.

"I'm still learning the strategy of running, I want to learn more and with this first year of cross country under my belt, I can gain so much for my future. My West Salem Coach, Tom Jimenez, and my mom tell me that I'm over thinking. I just need to stop thinking and run my race. A tremendous amount of pressure was put on me – I worked through that and had a successful season – I'm happy with the result," Brooke said.

When Brooke trains she doesn't run around her neighborhood, she prefers to run at the high school track. The start of her workout includes, jogging slowly to warm up. That's followed by running several 400 meters to improve her time on the 1500 meter run. She has also decided to add weightlifting to her training – this will strengthen her muscles.

As she grows and develops she will learn more about training the right way. She's only beginning her quest and is mysteriously gaining on her competition.

When Brooke receives a break from training she enjoys watching movies. Listening to pop music on her iPhone App is one of her favorite hobbies ... as long as it isn't Taylor Swift. She finds Taylor annoying with all of her breakup lyrics.

Brooke definitely knows what she wants. There was a time that she had a cross country meet in Albany, Oregon. It was the same day that an OSU football game was scheduled. The Interstate 5 freeway was normally packed with cars.

The Chuhlantseffs decided to drive there through the back road to prevent any traffic jam. About halfway to Albany, Brooke spoke up.

"Mom, I forgot my shoes! We have to go back to get them," Brooke expressed.

Brooke really insisted that she must have those shoes, sure enough Daniela turned around and drove back to the house. They picked up the shoes she wanted to run in and drove back to Albany. They just made it there in time for her to run – whew!

"That's just Brooke, everything has to be just right," Daniela said.

Every year Nike invites the top 40 runners (1A – 6A schools) from Oregon and from Washington to compete in the Nike Border Clash – Oregon girls against Washington girls. Brooke was invited since she was the ninth best in Oregon. Wow! What exciting news for this young lady.

On November 17th, 2012, Brooke and her family headed to Beaverton, Oregon, to register at the Tiger Woods Center.

"It was so amazing to see my daughter arrive at such a world-wide known place. Wow! The Nike World Headquarters Campus," Daniela said.

After Brooke had registered it was time for the mandatory course run-through with team captains at 3:00 p.m. When the run-through was completed it was shower time and get-dressed time from 4:00 p.m. to 5:00 p.m. An athletic activity would take place from 5:00 p.m. to 6:00 p.m. And finally to end the evening, dinner at the Nike World Headquarters Campus followed by a presentation.

Brooke was having the time of her life – a wonderful evening for a talented young lady. She was given Nike merchandise along with all the other athletes there. She received up to $300.00 (which is the legal limit) worth of merchandise including warm-ups, shirts, shoes, etc.

"It was a special evening and it was an honor to represent Oregon at the Nike Border Clash. It's always a great experience to run against the best," Brooke said.

Brooke placed 13th out of 80 girls that competed in this event. It was a huge deal for every girl that raced. And once again, Brooke was going up against seniors and juniors – it's easy for people to overlook that.

Brooke didn't receive much of a break between seasons because it was getting close to the track and field season. When the spring-sport season got going, Brooke was easily winning all of her local competition races. Her events were the 800 meter run and the 1500 meter run. She would also do the 3000 meter run at times.

Brooke was beginning to feel more comfortable having a coach in high school. Her coach, Tom Jimenez, knew that she was fast and also started to learn about her personality which made things easier for Brooke.

On April 12th, 2013 early in the track and field season, West Salem was headed to Canby, Oregon, to participate at the Canby Invitational. It was a cool cloudy evening with a threat of a light shower or sprinkle. The teams competing were, West Salem High School; Sprague High School; Kelso High School; Crescent Valley High School; Silverton High School; Tualitan High School; Battleground High School and Canby High School.

One of the top-ranked 800 meter runners in the state of Oregon was Aiyanna Cameron-Lewis who happened to be a junior this year. Crescent Valley was a lucky school to have such a talented runner. Unfortunately, Brooke was about to face a tough test early in the season.

During this meet Brooke was scheduled to only run the 800 meters. No 1500, or 3000 meters. The reason is unclear. Coaches make decisions that athletes have to honor at times.

As Brooke walked out on the track, she hopped up and down loosening up her legs. She was wearing orange running shoes, black socks, and black shorts with a black tank top. Her hair was tied up in a ponytail.

There was a pack of runners and Aiyanna was one of them. The official raised the gun, "Go to your marks!" The runners got on a ready stance, "Set!" There was a two-second pause ... bang! The gun went off and the runners sprinted from their marks. Right from the beginning Aiyanna and Brooke took the lead running head to head, except Brooke's head was about six inches shorter than Aiyanna's. Brooke is 5' 7" but from the stadium bleachers she looked six inches shorter than Aiyanna – definitely a long leg advantage. The 800 meters is a sprint anymore these days.

When you watched the two pull away from the rest of the pack you could obviously tell they were in a league of their own. Brooke was running a tight race against her competitor for the entire first lap. When the bell lap sounded the split was roughly 65 seconds for both girls. Midway through the second lap Brooke's breathing began to give her problems.

Her allergies hit hard at a bad time. Her times had been inconsistent because of this medical condition. Brooke had been battling what medication would work best for her. In the Willamette Valley, which is where Brooke lives – the pollination is terrible. In addition, Brooke was dealing with food allergies she did not know about at the time – not a great thing to be going through during an invitational track meet.

Brooke didn't complain about anything, she just ran her race the best she could. She was a fierce competitor and the medical issues would not keep her from running.

Aiyanna slowly gained the lead as Brooke fought the best she could to keep up. By the time they reached the finish line Brooke fell five yards behind – she just didn't have enough to catch Aiyanna. Aiyanna ran a 2:19.22 and Brooke ran a 2:23.02 – a very exciting race to watch. What was even more impressive was Brooke congratulating Aiyanna at the end of the race – a true sign of good sportsmanship.

Brooke has her sights on improving and learning as much as she can as a freshman. She is very young and has a competitive drive that will take her a long way. Her mom is someone anyone would love to have as a supporter. She definitely is one of the reasons that Brooke is able to continue following a dream.

During the track and field season some people were too hard on Brooke. Their expectations were too high simply because she was so talented. If she had a bad day at a meet, some people would overlook the fact that she was only a freshman and also that she was suffering from several allergies.

"Everyone has been so hard on her, as to why she hasn't performed better. Well, now we know. Living in the middle of a grass field doesn't help either. I wish people would just give her a break because regardless, she still hasn't done that bad," Daniela said.

Some of the situations that Brooke has run into have been rather stressful. One in particular was about some boys that seemed to be a little envious due to positive attention she was getting from the media.

"I never had any problems with the girls, but for some reason a few boys on my team would harass me. They would tell me that I was never going to make it to the state meet. They would bug me for no reason. In my frame of mind I was going to prove them wrong," Brooke said.

Brooke seemed to send her message across just fine. Before the district meet, she had won two first-place awards in the 1500 meters. On April 24th, 2012, she won at the McNary vs. West Salem meet with a time of 4:58.00. At the Nike/Jesuit Twilight Relays she won with a time of 4:48.16. She would soon have an opportunity to win another first place medal at the CVC District Meet.

Brooke continued to train hard. She realized that she needed to find what works best for her as far as running a good race.

"I have a lot to learn about racing stuff. I need to not go out too fast, and need to find a way to prevent myself from getting trapped inside the pack. I also need to stop thinking so much and just run my race. I've got four years of high school, so I have time. It takes time to improve," Brooke said.

On May 17th, 2012, it was time for the Central Valley Conference District Meet. First and second place finishers would advance to the OSAA Track and Field Championships in Eugene, Oregon, at Hayward Field – Track Town USA.

Track and field is such an exciting sport to watch. The running events and the field events make it a full day of entertainment and excitement. The weather in Oregon is always unpredictable, but on this day it was sunny and about 65 degrees.

Brooke's sister, Madison, and her mom show up early and sit on the left side of the stadium. They wait anxiously for the 1500 and 800 meter races. Madison is a fifth grader at Kalapuya Elementary School in West Salem – four years younger than Brooke. She has taken a liking to volleyball – playing the setter position. She also likes running ... just like Brooke.

"I'm doing great as far as a runner. I want to be just like my sister – she's amazing. I run a lot because I want to get better. Brooke has inspired me to work hard. I think I can get a college scholarship if I work hard enough," Madison said.

The time has finally come, the 1500 meter race is about to start. Brooke wears number 243 on her black track uniform. She's wearing pink running shoes and looks very relaxed. The gun sounds and the runners start moving fast down the stretch. Brooke starts out in front and increases her lead by ten yards from the pack. The second lap she is now 20 yards ahead of everyone else – juniors and seniors included. The third lap this young freshman has increased the lead by 30 yards. Brooke wins ahead of the pack by 50 yards and her time is 4:51.09. She becomes the CVC District Champion in the 1500 meter run! She also went on to win the 800 meters.

Brooke advanced to the 6A OSAA State Track and Field Championships in Eugene, Oregon. She placed 11th in the 1500 meter run and just missed the finals in the 800 meter run.

"I found myself trapped inside the pack at the state meet. It was like a maze that I could not get out of. The other girls were also stronger than I was. I'm frustrated because of my times – I know I'm more capable. I'm definitely working harder to prepare for next year," Brooke said.

A successful season is an understatement for this young lady who has the determination to improve every year. She has visions of becoming the state champion by her senior year of high school or sooner. Brooke has received 26 letters from different colleges, USC; Colorado; Montana; Washington; Stanford; U of Oregon and more.

Daniela has some words of advice for parents who have kids following a dream like Brooke. She has experienced plenty supporting her daughter. She has shown how much she loves her daughter by her actions – simply caring.

"Don't ever decide for them which sport they need to do. You have to encourage your child to continue reaching their dream. It's their life and we are the supporters behind them. I think it's horrible that some parents don't let their kids do sports – so many things they learn," Daniela said.

Some people may not know that Brooke is a self-driven competitor and is full of dedication in whatever she does. She has a drive to accomplish all things – nobody makes her do anything. She just has that "Mom let's go!" attitude.

"My goal is to win state by my senior year. I want to make it to the 2016 Olympic Trials. A college scholarship is definitely in my plans. Maintaining a 4.0 GPA would be amazing and maybe someday go into the field of Animal Science or Marine Biology," Brooke said.

The future is so bright for Brooke Chuhlantseff. Her hard work has paid off and her planning for the future is set on the right track. Brooke is an inspiring story for young athletes. She will go a long way in the sport of track and field. Who knows, we may see her at the 2016 Olympic Trials. Great job setting a positive mark Brooke!

Daniel Brattain Has Hurdle Heights to Reach

The hurdles have to be one of the toughest events to master in track and field. To excel takes a combination of precise technique and speed. This event requires a graceful-three-step rhythm as a runner sprints off the blocks, hoping to not hit a hurdle for the best finish time possible. I was so impressed when I first watched this young man run a hurdle race as a freshman in high school.

Daniel Brattain was born in Tualitan, Oregon, at Meridian Park Hospital, on November 13, 1995. His parents are Rob and Rhonda. Rob manages the Salem branch of his family-owned business, Brattain International Trucks – he still continues to manage that branch. Rob is also a pilot in the Army National Guard and has been deployed three times throughout the years.

Rhonda was a realtor when the kids were little but is now a homemaker and the Booster Club President at McNary High School. She has been like a single parent due to being an army wife. It's a tough life with four kids.

"When Rob started getting deployed for different missions, I was the only one that could take the kids to school – I had to be there for our kids. That ended my real estate profession," Rhonda said.

Daniel almost died before he was born. When Rhonda was expecting Daniel she had gone in to the hospital thinking it was time. She was informed that she needed to go home because it wasn't quite time yet. Rhonda disagreed with the hospital staff. She did not want to go home because she felt something was wrong with the baby.

"I felt a sciatic nerve pain down the side of my leg. I felt something was wrong. I refused to go home. It's a good thing I trusted my instincts, because I don't know what I would have done without Daniel – he has been a blessing," Rhonda said.

The doctors discovered that Daniel had what you call nuchal cord. This is a condition where the umbilical cord is wrapped around the baby's neck. A cesarean section is usually required to prevent any harm to the baby.

If Rhonda would have gone home that day, she could have lost Daniel to stillbirth or possibly risk other damages to his body. During the prenatal period, he would not have suffered from suffocation, since the umbilical cord is what provides the oxygen before birth.

Daniel was raised in a low-income neighborhood. He has one younger sister, Charlotte, and two older brothers, Michael and James. Daniel was always trying to keep up with his older brothers – trying to outdo them in just about any running or jumping game they played.

His mom talks about a ceiling board that was about nine feet tall. His brothers would have marks on it to indicate how high they stamped their hands on it. Daniel reached that mark at a very young age.

They would play running games and again Daniel would work so hard to win. He was just a natural-born competitor – willing to do anything to win.

When Daniel was little he struggled with speech problems. Rhonda took him to a special speech school. This school was good to him. They would take the students on field trips. One trip they took was to the fire station – Daniel loved this.

"He would tell me that he was going to do that – be a fireman. It didn't matter what it was, he wanted to do that. He had a lot of drive on wanting to do everything," Rhonda said.

He was such an active kid that all of his ambition during those years developed him into a physically-fast individual.

His dad, Rob, worked at the airfield. Daniel loved going there. The staff adopted him because he was always around asking questions and exploring. There was a time that Daniel even broke one of the helicopters. He was observing the chopper. He grabbed the latch thinking it was how you open the door. Unfortunately it was the emergency latch – as he pulled it, the entire door fell off!

In 1999, when Charlotte was a baby, the family moved to a middle-income-class area in Keizer, Oregon. Daniel would attend Willamette Valley Christian School in Brooks, Oregon, kindergarten through fourth grade. He then made a transition to Clearlake Elementary School in Keizer.

This was a very difficult transition for the kids. They had been sheltered for a big part of their life. Clearlake is a public school – a tough adjustment to make for the Brattains.

Daniel was the type of kid that would stand up for any kid that got bullied. He got into trouble one time because he stepped in on a bully that was picking on a small kid.

"Daniel got right into this big kid's face and started an altercation. He just didn't like innocent kids getting bullied," Rhonda said.

The principal told Daniel that it was school policy to not fight. But at the same time he told Daniel that he did the right thing. School policies had to be carried out for standard procedures. This made Daniel feel relieved that he really wasn't in any trouble because of what he had done.

Daniel sometimes felt that his peers didn't take him serious at times. If he informed some students of certain things, he felt that they didn't believe him. They would often say that he was lying or making things up.

"It really bothered me that some kids didn't believe what I was saying at times when it was the real truth," Daniel said.

School was challenging for Daniel, sometimes his grades would drop, and he would joke around in class – goof off at times. Rhonda had to step in and talk to him various times about different situations. Slowly things got resolved – parenting can be challenging at times.

Daniel had several friends during the elementary school days, Cort Peetz, Josiah Kneel, Jordan Smith and Caleb Peet. Caleb is someone that he has remained friends with to this current day.

"Caleb and I have always been friends. He's someone that I can relate to. We hang out together whenever we can.

I enjoy having him as a true friend – he supports me and I support him," Daniel said.

Daniel is not only a track and field athlete, but he also plays the French horn and the saxophone. His mom would have loved for him to continue playing this instrument and for him to someday play in college, but it just wasn't what Daniel wanted to do.

"My mom was pushing me a little too much on the instruments. It wasn't fun playing back then, but now that she has backed off, I now enjoy it more," Daniel said.

Parents want the best for their kids, and sometimes it's easy to forget when a parent enjoys something so much and wants their child to follow in the same footsteps. But Rhonda realized that immediately and allowed Daniel to follow his own dream.

"We just want our kids to be happy, it's up to them to choose whatever they want to do. It's our job to support them," Rhonda said.

Daniel was involved in many activities during middle school. One time he went down to the Salem Saturday Market and played the saxophone for two hours. He wanted to raise money for Relay for Life (Cancer research, etc.) He also did that for a baseball fundraiser and a track and field fundraiser.

"We have so many talented musicians that enjoy playing sports as well. I think they should be able to do both. But there is a conflict because you can't do Jazz Band unless you're in Concert Band. So naturally a lot of the boys will choose to play football, basketball, or track and field.

This forces them to choose one over the other. It seems like they should be able to do both if they want," Rhonda said.

I have to agree with Rhonda on this one. There's also a conflict with the Drama Department. It would be great if students could do both, drama and sports. It's a really good combination to have. This is something I feel schools really need to address – but maybe because of the amount of practice time it takes for both, it's not possible.

Daniel's life as a young kid was very depressing at times. The third time his dad was deployed to Iraq, he was gone an entire year. Previous to that he was gone six months and nine months. When Rob was home he was working at his family business. He was supporting his family financially, but to a young kid, it's always a difficult thing to understand.

"When my dad was gone, I cried a lot. I missed having a dad around. Sometimes I couldn't think. I understood that he was supporting our family financially, but it was very painful. I tried to put all of the emotions into my running and workout," Daniel said.

When Rob was home he always encouraged Daniel to do the best he could at anything he did. Rob actually did not know how fast Daniel really was. He would find out once Daniel reached high school.

It's difficult to know if that had something to do with Daniel's behavior issues at school from time to time. There were instances where the teacher would complain about Daniel goofing off in class or trying to be funny.

Daniel's parents would take privileges away when he got into trouble with teachers at school. Some said that he was talking too much during class.

"I just took his cell phone away, or things he enjoyed doing. I told him that grades were important, especially if he wanted to go to college someday," Rhonda said.

Daniel started attending Whiteaker Middle School in Keizer, his life was about to change. The track coaches were very impressed when they saw how fast Daniel was. Scott Coburn was one of the P.E. teachers and the track coach. The other P.E. teacher, Mrs. Biamont, was the one that showed Daniel the basic technique for the hurdles. Daniel fell in love with this event – he was a natural at it.

"When I got to sixth grade I was running a hurdle race against Justin Burgess, an eighth grader that I admired because of his athleticism. I remember the gun sounding and Justin taking off like a flash. I started pushing hard after the third hurdle and before I realized it, I was right next to Justin. He helped me tie the school record. Justin inspired me to become a great hurdler. That's also when I first realized that I had a special gift in running the hurdles. After that moment I started practicing hard to be the best I could be. I continued working with Mrs. Biamont to improve in my hurdle technique," Daniel said.

Sometimes that's what it takes, going out and trying something, we don't know how things will turn out, but the important thing is that we try. With Daniel, he had discovered that he was built to be a hurdler.

"All I heard from the coaches was, 'Have you seen your son run?' Parents and students would also inform me about how fast Daniel was," Rhonda said.

Rhonda told her husband about all of this. She often talked to him about what was going on with the kids since he was not home most of the time. He worked a lot with his business and the Army National Guard.

"Wow, I didn't know Daniel was fast – that is very cool!" Rob said.

Rob was not a feely-touchy kind of person – he loved Daniel from inside his heart. Being away from Daniel and his kids was very hard for him. When a person is committed to the Army, the orders arrive and the brave men or women have to comply with the Army. No questions asked.

"I think it was hardest on Charlotte, my little girl – the youngest. I understood how Daniel must have felt – it was hard on all of us," Rob said.

Rhonda was close to Daniel, she would have breakfast with him on a regular basis. She did so many things for him and spent countless hours keeping up with him. Their relationship was amazing – Rhonda loved Daniel very much and was very proud of him.

Daniel went on to break the middle school record in the hurdles his seventh grade year. This was just a matter of time. He loved running the hurdles, it became his passion in track and field. Daniel also played basketball and football.

Many hours were spent practicing the lead leg over the hurdle and then the trail leg following with a snap. The objective was to get as close to the hurdle without touching it, that way you're running the hurdle and not jumping it.

When he enrolled at McNary High School, in Keizer, Oregon, there was something about a first impression. He was attending daily doubles at the beginning of football season. There was a kid that was giving him a bunch of crap. It was starting to annoy Daniel so much that he finally put his foot down.

"This kid thought he was faster than everyone, and had a bad attitude. He kept bugging me about many things. I finally pulled him over after practice one day. I told him that as long as we were on the same team I was not going to fight him. We are teammates and should support each other. After the football season was over, if he still wanted to fight me, I would do it then," Daniel said.

The kid took Daniel's words seriously and they actually became friends during the football season. Sometimes communicating is the answer to a lot of kids that have issues among each other. Daniel did the right thing, except for the fight part, but I think that's just a young-high-school kid standing up for what he believed in.

Daniel never seemed to have an issue with girls being around him. According to his mom, he had different girlfriends throughout the years. Some were just friends and others were his actual girlfriends.

"My mom doesn't really know what goes on with the girls I'm around, she just says things. I have a friend, her name is Lexi – we're just friends," Daniel said.

Daniel has come to knowing who he is in high school. He doesn't like talking to the know-it-all popular kids. He doesn't feel comfortable around kids that feel they're better than everyone else. Not saying that all popular kids are like that, but they do exist in just about any high school. And then again, we all have faults – some of us have more than others.

"I know the type of kids that Daniel talks about. Some of these kids are very talented athletes. It's very sad to see someone that has so much potential in athletics make poor decisions," Rhonda said.

Daniel was involved in several programs, not just Young Life, but also Campaigners, a group that met Wednesday mornings to pray before school.

Jeremy Williams (Willy) was a Young Life leader. He was a great father figure for Daniel when Rob was deployed for a year. Jeremy took Daniel to coffee places – they talked and just hung out together. Daniel enjoyed that so much and got used to it. Unfortunately Willy moved on to work with college kids and left the McNary area – a tough situation for Daniel.

"When Jeremy left, it just broke me. I felt empty inside. No dad around and now the father-figure person I used to hang out with ... gone. I would be in my room filled with sadness. It was a tough time for me – I just didn't think life was fair," Daniel explained as tears ran down his eyes.

Daniel worked through his emotions and found energy to continue working out. The hurdles were a great outlet to pour out everything emotionally. At McNary this young kid would begin to set marks as soon as he stepped into the high school track.

The coaches had recognized him at Whiteaker Middle School. They filled him with encouragement and looked forward to having him in high school. According to Rhonda, his hurdle coach, Ken Scott, was going to leave McNary until he saw Daniel coming into the track and field program. He decided to stay at McNary and work with Daniel. He saw the natural talent in this athlete – what coach would not want to hang around and see success accomplished by his student. The Brattains were thankful that Coach Scott hung around for a few more years.

Daniel Brattain Has Hurdle Heights to Reach

Daniel was getting ready for high school track. He would go out to the track by himself to work on the hurdles. He knew that the height of a hurdle in high school was higher than the 30 inches in middle school. In high school the standard height is 39 inches high. What he didn't know was that the hurdles he was practicing on were set at 42 inches – college heights. I'd say that was much higher than high school heights. Daniel was struggling, hitting them and tripping as he tried jumping instead of running over them – falling down time after time.

"He kept coming home and telling me that he wasn't going to be able to do this in high school. The hurdles were just too high. And I would try to encourage him to keep at it," Rhonda said.

One day Coach Scott saw Daniel practicing and he noticed the hurdle height. He instantly notified Daniel that he had them set at the wrong height. They needed to be 39 inches high.

"I was so relieved when he adjusted them to the correct height, it was much better and I could actually clear them pretty easy," Daniel laughs.

"Coach Scott was good for Daniel – he taught him so much about the hurdle technique. He is a great hurdle coach. We are very thankful to him for all the work he has done with Daniel," Rhonda said.

Sometimes coaches get so focused on what they want out of an athlete that it's easy to forget what the athlete wants. We can go back to letting the kid decide what he wants to do and not anyone else. Supporting them in what they choose to do. Parents sometimes fall into this as well as coaches.

"I have enjoyed Coach Scott and am thankful for all of his help. But I do disagree with some of his opinions. I feel that I should be allowed to work on the required field events to improve at being a decathlete someday. I really like my coach, but we just have different views," Daniel said.

Daniel's relationship with his coach is good as far as hurdles. The coach is looking out for the program, the team, and for the event he coaches. Daniel is looking out for his future as a hurdler and a decathlete. He would love to do the decathlon in college in the future. But he feels that he has been hindered by not getting much opportunity to develop during track practice. This is a good argument on both parts – and something to think about.

Daniel's solution has been training in Oregon City with an organization called the Willamette Striders. They have an indoor facility that he can use to practice – especially for the pole vault. It just makes it tougher for him to travel an hour away to get practice in.

Along with all of that, Daniel faced yet another distraction. His older brother James was one he always looked up to and idolized. He wanted to be like James – always following him around as a little kid. He wanted to be as good as him in the sports world ... and in everything basically. James, Michael, and Daniel would compete in everything – all kinds of running and jumping games.

Then one day James started making bad decisions in life. This really hurt Daniel. It was hard for him to focus and he knew he could not follow his brother on the things he was doing.

Daniel was emotionally drained again, but continued working out – this was like counseling for him. Running is such a great stress reliever – a great balance to have if anyone is going through rough times like Daniel was.

"With all the things that went on in my life, the person I really missed was my granddad down in Florida. He meant the world to me. I used to have so much fun with him. Growing up he took me fishing and taught me all kinds of things. He lives in the country – I have learned to love the country. Every summer we would go there to visit. Now he has major health problems and I'm deeply saddened," Daniel tilts his head down.

Daniel had been close to his granddad for years. His relationship was so close that when Daniel talks about him, it brings him to tears. There are so many good memories he had with his granddad growing up – it continues to this day.

"Daniel's granddad, Ronald McGill, has a spine problem that has gotten worse over the years. He is stubborn and wants to live by himself in the country – the house he's always lived in. We brought him to Oregon once to give him the opportunity to watch Daniel run the hurdles. That was such a joy for him to see his grandson win a race. He always brags on Daniel to all of his friends and family back in Florida. He is very proud of Daniel," Rhonda said.

After Daniel's granddad returned to Florida, the young hurdler started feeling like he now had a reason to run. His reason was his granddad. After he saw how delighted the sixty-eight-year-old man was, it was not too difficult to work harder at his quest. He wants to make his granddad proud – he enjoyed seeing the smiles he brought to his granddad.

"We really would have loved to move my dad to Oregon, but while he was visiting, he about froze to death. Oregon and Florida are opposite when it comes to weather," Rhonda said.

Daniel was excelling in the hurdles, dominating the local competitions. As a freshman he had earned a ranking as one of the top hurdlers in the Central Valley Conference. In the spring of 2011 he was getting ready to compete in the 6A CVC District Meet at North Salem High School. Six schools were competing, McNary; North Salem; West Salem; Sprague; McKay and South Salem.

Most competitors get nervous right before the actual race. Daniel gets nervous the night before. He tries to visualize the explosion take off from the blocks – that seems to help a lot.

"During the actual race, I'm at the starting line with my hands down on the track waiting for the gun to sound. I take a deep breath and hold it until the gun sounds – bang! I breathe out and take off. That helps me attack the first hurdle with strong velocity. As I run over each hurdle I focus on the object past the finish line," Daniel said.

At the CVC District Track Meet I showed up early and I saw Daniel. This was a kid that used to play basketball at the open gyms. My son, Matt Espinoza, was the head basketball coach at McNary during that time and he would allow Daniel to come play as an eighth grader. That's how I know Daniel, but I had no idea he ran the hurdles. So this meet was more meaningful to me now. He was very polite to me and I wished him good luck – I would be cheering for him to do well.

It was finally time for the 110 high hurdles to begin. When the gun sounded, three hurdlers took the lead from the start, they were attacking the hurdles. This couldn't be, a freshman in high school three-stepping the hurdles all the way through. That is very rare. Daniel opened my eyes with his natural God-given talent.

He stood at about 6' 1" and was race-horse slender. He was fast and graceful. The rhythm between hurdles was amazing. Daniel took second, losing by inches to a kid from South Salem High School. Wow, I was totally impressed with the race he lost to a senior. This is the reason I am writing his story, because I call it a northwest success story. I knew by watching him for the first time, that he had a great future ahead of him.

Daniel went on to place ninth at the OSAA State Track and Field Championships in Eugene, Oregon, which were held at Hayward Field – Track Town USA.

"At the state meet, it was all different. I didn't get to warm up as much as I would have liked to. Staging areas were very formal, and then of course by the time they brought us out to the track I wasn't as prepared. The enormous crowd was a little nerve racking for me being so young – a great learning experience though," Daniel said.

One of the most memorable moments for Daniel was during his sophomore year at the CVC District Championships. Daniel broke the school record and the district meet record with a time of 14.69. Although he runs the 300 meters hurdles and has great times in that race, the 110 highs are definitely his passion.

"When I saw him running over each hurdle, I was so nervous, but I knew how hard he had worked for this and how much he wanted to break the record – and he did it! His dad and I were so proud to be there witnessing the whole thing," Rhonda said with a smile.

His sophomore year, Daniel ran a 14.69 to take first place. Brandon Fletcher, from West Salem, ran a 15.81 to take the second state qualifying spot.
Daniel went on to place fourth at the OSAA 6A State Championships as a sophomore. Every year he seems to be improving – he is a very determined athlete.

"Breaking the 15 second barrier as a freshman was one of my great moments, but my best moment had to be breaking the school record and the district record with a time of 14.69. All of the hard work that I put in over the years paid off. It's such a great feeling," Daniel said.

Daniel overcame several obstacles on the way, emotional incidents and many other things. He dealt with all of them the best he could. And despite all of that, he managed to earn a huge award – a record for the fastest time.
Daniel has a great future ahead of him – he maintains a 3.8 GPA in the academic world and has plans of possibly attending the Air Force Academy. It's like West Point (Army). He wants to play football as well, he loves the cornerback position. Track and field is definite – decathlon and hurdles. He's still juggling the idea of what to do for his future. He also wants to slowly build a home in Florida where his granddad lives, he loves the country there. He believes he's destined to be there someday.
Rhonda has some advice for parents who have a child that might be following a dream like Daniels. She says the dream should come from the kid not the adult. Once the child finds something they have a passion for, the parents should support and encourage their child all they can. The day-to-day actions should be "keep them practicing." Be

there for them when they are also not doing well. And if you can afford it, sign them up for private lessons – it does help tremendously.

"We are all proud of Daniel, no matter what he ends up being," Rhonda said.

Daniel has set a mark at McNary High School as one of the best hurdlers ever to attend there. Great job Daniel and the best of luck in the future!

Brittney Kiser, a Swimmer Despite Emotional Hardship

Some girls that are involved in sports face more emotional stress than others. I take great pleasure to share a story of a courageous young lady who loves swimming and would love to compete in college some day. Her road has been full of challenging obstacles.

Brittney Kiser was born in Salem, Oregon, at Salem Hospital, on September 24, 1997. Her parents are Scott and Tara. She has two brothers, Jon and Tim.

Scott was a fourth-grade teacher at Myers Elementary School in Salem and still teaches there. Tara was also an elementary teacher and continues as well – she teaches at Harritt Elementary School.

Brittney was born late, but had not received nutrients for the last few months before her birth. She was very small and underdeveloped. They discovered she had a heart murmur (blood flow that produces an audible sound). There are different types of heart murmurs. She would have ongoing checkups to monitor this condition. Time was the case and eventually the heart murmur would not show up anymore.

Brittney grew up in a middle-income-class Christian family. The neighborhood was calm. In fact, the Kisers' house was the first one built in their subdivision. As families moved in, Brittney and her brothers would play baseball, football and just about any outdoor game with mostly boys. She was the middle child and according to her mom, definitely a tomboy. Brittney was not a little girl that would play with dolls. She liked to play outside with the boys – all kinds of sports-activity games.

"We kept hoping there would be other families that moved in with kids in Brittney's age group, but most of the families that were building homes in our area had older siblings," Scott said.

This young lady loved to swim in their backyard pool. Something started her swimming adventures and a drive that kept her competing in the pool.

"My mom inspired me to become a swimmer – she used to be a swimmer back in the days. She signed me up for swimming lessons at Olinger Pool in Salem. I didn't do that great on my first race, but it got better every time," Brittney said.

Brittney was ten years old when her mom suggested they go to the Courthouse Athletic Club to get involved with a swim team. Brittney was delighted and looked forward to the fun experience.

"She's definitely an outdoor kid that likes to be active. She's also artistic, loves to draw pictures, and was always autographing her name in just about everything," Tara laughs.

The Kiser parents never told their kids what they should do as far as sports. With Brittney, they introduced dancing to her. That lasted a day – they knew she was not interested in that. Her dad, Scott, is a musician that plays an instrument and sings for his church. Music is definitely something Brittney was interested in, so they encouraged and supported her.

It's always nice to have other hobbies when you're an athlete that trains for a sport – especially a sport like swimming. In Brittney's case, she enjoyed music as well.

"My friend, Maddy Potloff and I started this band called 'Bad.' I was really into music. We hung out together a lot and just had fun. One time we went on a cruise with my parents. We had the opportunity to perform in a talent show. We sung "Best of Both Worlds," a Hannah Montana song. We actually received an award!" Brittney said.

Brittney attended Gubser Elementary School in Keizer, Oregon. When she was in fifth grade she transferred to Myers Elementary School in West Salem. Salem and Keizer are two cities next to each other in Oregon. Her dad was a teacher at Myers and things worked out a lot better for them.

Part of growing up is discovering things and learning from experiences. Brittney was getting into a little trouble at times during school. At Myers Elementary, Scott had a network of friends – word got to him really fast. This kept Brittney on the right track.

"Yeah, it didn't take long before the students at Myers found out I was Mr. Kiser's daughter. I guess there was something about the last name that gave it away. My dad even suggested not saying anything when I first got there. He wanted to see how long it would take before people found out – they found out instantly," Brittney smiles.

Swimming began to be Brittney's enjoyment and passion. She started developing a special technique in the backstroke. That was putting her as one of the top swimmers in her age group in the local area.

The backstroke may seem easy when you watch an expert swimmer taking action, but there are many technical components to this style. Some people know it as the back crawl or the upside-down freestyle.

Let's start with the advantages verses other types of swimming strokes. Breathing is easier with the backstroke, since you're facing upward in the water. You also start a race in the water with your legs up on the wall – no diving. The disadvantages are, not being able to see where you're going and being disqualified for touching the wall before you flip previous to the final stretch.

"In the 100 yard backstroke, the first fifty yards I count my strokes and I keep an eye on the flags above – that lets me know I'm getting close to the wall. If I touch the wall at the end of the first fifty yards, I would be disqualified. The final fifty yards, I go all out and when I touch the wall, my entire body stops. I've hurt my wrist a few times hitting the wall," Brittney said.

The technique for the backstroke is pretty amazing. Brittney has to take long axis strokes (one arm is stiff in the air) while the other arm is doing its job landing in the water. As the hand hits the water it's turned to slice the H20 and prevent resistance. The same hand is then used to push off for more speed. The legs are constantly fluttering. The entire body must be stabilized for the best result. Brittney's upper body strength along with her technique helps her in this race.

This young brunette realized she had talent in middleschool. She was competing in a lot of club swim meets. She received a lot of first place awards in the backstroke. In some meets she would come from behind to win a race.

"We always went to her swim meets, we never missed one. We were always there supporting our daughter and cheering her on," Tara said.

Her parents speak of the support they gave to her during the swimming season – and that is a great thing. But sometimes during the off season they would go on vacations.
Brittney speaks of missing her parents when they were gone. Her mom would win cruises from her home décor business. This was very difficult for Brittney – she missed her parents – she did not want them to be gone for such a long time.

"I remember sitting on the steps one time ... crying and pleading with them not to go. I didn't want them to go – I wanted them to stay home. They would bring us presents when they returned to make us feel better. My grandparents took care of us while Mom and Dad were gone on vacations. Allen and Jean Kiser would watch us half of the week. Tom and Lora Halferty would watch us the second half of the week. I love my grandparents they were always there to help out," Brittney said.

Brittney thinks highly of her grandparents, both sides. They would bring the kids snacks and spend time with them while their parents were gone. They would tutor Brittney with whatever she was struggled with that was school related.
Scott and Tara vacationed a lot but they always made sure their kids were taken care of. They took advantage of

free cruises and enjoyed the breaks from the daily work they took on.

Brittney's relationship with her mom was not the greatest for a long time. They were always at each others' nerves. It was hard for them to communicate with each other. One might see it as a personality difference, or maybe just a mother-daughter regular experience.

"I love Brittney, but sometimes she would be so moody and it was difficult to talk to her about anything – she was definitely a daddy's girl. She enjoyed doing a lot of things with her dad," Tara says.

Brittney definitely agrees with her mom about being a daddy's girl. She would join in on outings like hunting, fishing, and anything else her dad did. She enjoyed shooting guns or baiting her own hook on a fishing trip.

"My mom would do stuff that irritated me. She would comb my hair and almost pull it out. It hurt so badly. That got me angry. Sometimes I would say that I hated her," Brittney said.

In 2004, Brittney's mom, Tara, was diagnosed with Multiple Sclerosis. MS is an inflammatory disease in which the insulation covers of the nerve cells in the brain and spinal cord are damaged. This causes problems with parts of the nervous system to communicate – resulting in a wide range of symptoms. For example, there were times when Tara could not walk. She started all kinds of treatments that helped a lot.

She chose to stay home with the kids for ten years and then returned to teaching – she managed well. MS is a struggle for her every day but she is a fighter.

"When Brittney found out about her mom's diagnosis, she asked me, 'Could Mom die from this?' I took one long look at her and said ... yes," Scott said.

Brittney's relationship with her mom instantly changed. She got closer to her and has started going on walks with her to spend more time together.

"It has gotten a lot better for both of us, I'm truly blessed to have a daughter like Brittney," Tara said.

Tara talks about Brittney being kind of like a third son. She loves spending time with her dad – she never really liked doing girly stuff.

"She's my princess – we love to do things together no matter what it is. When the boyfriend comes home ... watch out," Scott says laughing.

While she practiced swimming three times a week, other challenges off the pool would be something she had to deal with. Reading has always been a struggle for Brittney – she suffers from dyslexia. There are different types. Brittney is believed to possibly suffer from primary dyslexia. With this type of dyslexia the reading is usually easier at the fourth or fifth grade level, even when she becomes a high school student or an adult. The brain translates the image differently as the eyes view the words.
It's very difficult for Brittney to read books with intellectual words. Teachers have given her oral tests for this reason. This is something she has to deal with every day. Brittney is a very bright individual and retains information (she hears) very well.
Teachers would eventually give her oral exams in school – it helped tremendously. She refuses to give up and

keeps working at different ways to make the grades. She would love to eventually bring her GPA up to 3.5 – for now she maintains a 2.9. Studying is difficult for her and the homework can be a nightmare. Her dream is to swim in college someday, and she's starting to realize that grades are super important.

"It's so hard for me to read books that are beyond fifth grade level, and I'm in high school now. My teachers are starting to give me oral exams, it's been helping me a lot," Brittney said.

The way this young lady trains might be a little different than most. She spends time in the pool of course, but when she's not in the pool, you can find her going on five-mile hikes – uphill and downhill. Her mom and dad also take her to Portland several times a year to do the 4T (Trail, Tram, Trolley and Train).

The 4T begins with a hike on the Marquam Trail to the city's highest point, Council Crest. You pass through the Oregon Health Science University campus. Then you ride the Portland Aerial Tram to the South Waterfront District. You hop on the streetcar (trolley) to cruise into downtown Portland. And finally, you return to the start via MAX light-rail train. The hike part of this adventure is steep and challenging – makes a great workout.

Brittney speaks highly of Hannah Russell, her number one friend. She also has other good friends she hangs out with, Tiffany Barba and Scott Bridger. Scott was a national champion in bowling. She also has a friend from California, Alex, who she keeps in contact with as well.

"I like hanging out with my friends. They understand me – we have a lot of fun together," Brittney said.

One of Brittney's favorite moments was when her club swim team won a meet in Turner, Oregon. The nickname for the team was "The Dream Team" that consisted of Angelian, Aryianna, Brooke and Brittney.

"That was the best team ever, we had a talented group of swimmers to win in the finals," Brittney said.

Brittney had always had an interest in being involved with the trainer during football season. She enjoyed assisting on the sidelines during a football game or during practices. In the fall of 2012, a terrible thing happened to Brittney. This would change her life and create anxiety and fear for a long time.

A seventeen-year-old boy, who she knew, and that attended her church, made a bad decision. It happened in the training room. She was sexually abused and taken advantage of by this boy.

"I said no five times," Brittney said.

The Kiser family was shocked by this and it created a huge disruption for the entire family. Brittney had nightmares – she even went to counseling. It created a fear in her that was very difficult to get through. When something like this happens to young girls it affects them for their entire life if they don't seek help. Even if they seek help, in most cases it commonly remains a scar for life.

Brittney could no longer do a lot of the things she used to. She feared that this boy would be there. She had thoughts of suicide at times. She attended meetings with her family and the church pastor. She continues to deal with this matter every day – some days are better than others.

"I was really angry when this happened to my little girl, I'm sure glad I didn't have my gun at the time – I probably would have been in prison," Scott said.

Time heals and the Kisers have gotten to be a closer family because of this ordeal. They all care so much about Brittney and would do anything to help her feel safe.

Brittney found strength within her. Her faith carried her through a rough time. God doesn't do this to young girls. When Jesus died for our sins he gave us free will. People make bad choices in this corrupt world and have repercussions to pay. God will guide this family, especially Brittney. I know my prayers go out to them.

The mental strength she had was what helped her continue with swimming. The high school season was about to start and she stepped up to the plate.

Swimming in high school verses middle school is tougher. Brittney has learned that the coaches push you more and encourage you to work harder than you ever have before. Her high school coach is Kim Phillips. Brittney has learned plenty from Kim and likes the high school swimming environment.

Brittney was a type of person that cared deeply for animals – doesn't like to see them sick or hurt. She took care of them when she felt they needed it. Her pet is a big black cat that she named Nelson Alexander Kiser – she adores him.

She also cared for little kids. She would go to her swimming workouts at the Courthouse Athletic Club. Afterward, she would stay and help the younger kids with their swimming technique – or just help them learn how to swim and encourage them. She always had a smile on her face.

One time during a P.E. class, there was a little girl that got injured. Brittney carried her all the way to the office so she could be treated. Not too many high school kids would go out of their way to help someone like that.

Brittney has received many awards during her young life. She has received a varsity letter as a freshman; bronze medal in state for bowling; volunteer award; good behavior award; best singer at Myers; honor choir and honor roll. These are just a few well earned awards, but I'm sure she will rack them up in the near future. With her positive outlook and hard work, plus her parents support, how can she go wrong?

To help herself keep up with studies she has been involved in the Avid Program (college prep program). She has also visited two colleges, George Fox University in Newberg, Oregon, and the University of Oregon, in Eugene.

"To be honest with you, we know that our daughter isn't going to be an Olympian or a professional swimmer – just being realistic. We're here to support her and encourage her so she can possibly swim in college someday. I wish that we could afford the lessons and other swim clubs that some of the kids are involved in, but we just can't afford that," Tara said.

During the swim season, at McNary High School, Brittney injured her ankle. She was out for a few days recovering. When she healed and was ready to return, the coach moved her from the varsity position down to the JV position.

"I was really upset when that happened. I didn't understand why I couldn't return to my spot on the varsity team. On JV none of the girls supported me when I was competing. If they were done with their race, they just left. On the varsity team it wasn't like that at all," Brittney said.

Sometimes coaches do things to help the team. It's always difficult for the athlete to understand why certain decisions are made.

"I like to use different girls for different events. I tried to rotate all of the girls so that some could race varsity at times. It also had to do with who we were swimming against. Brittney's strength is definitely the backstroke – she's amazing and has so much potential. I really don't think she knows how good she could be," Kim Phillips said.

Brittney was an impact right away, winning swim races – it wasn't long before the varsity coach moved her back up to the team. It wasn't the same for Brittney – she belonged with the best swimmers at McNary. She also did what she was told with not too much complaining.
Jon and Tim, her brothers have been very supportive of Brittney. They don't envy her at all. They are both happy that she is doing well in swimming and other sports like bowling. Her brother Jon will be attending Chemeketa Community College for free. He earned a GPA better than 3.5 which will qualify him for free tuition.
Brittney would love to follow her brother's footsteps and possibly transfer to a university after two years at Chemeketa.

"We've always taught our kids to support one another, we're proud of all three no matter what they choose to do. We want to be parents that bust our tails in encouraging them and supporting them with their activities – we've never known differently," Scott said.

The Kiser family volunteers every year with the concessions at McNary High School. They are heavily involved with the booster club. The parents have set an example for their kids to help the community and be involved. The family has received a Volunteer of the Year Award – that takes some doing.

Having an athlete in the family like Brittney, who has dreams of swimming on a college team someday, has made the parents and brothers proud to be a part of it.

"It's an awesome feeling to have a daughter that's so talented in the backstroke. We don't want to be too proud, but we're very proud of her. Sometimes we just think, 'There's Brittney, our daughter!' She's a real blessing to us," Scott said.

During the winter season the swim races are in yards and during the summer season the races are in meters. All of Brittney's races would have been in yards. Varsity Head Coach Kim Phillips had Brittney race the 100 yard free style and the 100 yard backstroke consistently. Sometimes she would use Brittney in the 200 yard medley relay and in the 200 yard freestyle relay. According to Kim it just depended on who was doing well during practices and what school McNary was competing against.

In February 2013, at the Kroc Center in Salem, it was time for the Central Valley Conference District Meet. The young freshman would compete against seniors and juniors. The schools competing in the CVC League were, McNary; Sprague; McKay; South Salem; North Salem and West Salem. It would be a two-day swim meet starting on Friday with the preliminaries.

Coach Phillips entered Brittney with her backstroke time of 1:21.1 – all athletes had to be formally entered into this competition with a time.

On Friday, the first day of the district swim meet, Brittney was ready to swim against some tough swimmers. She doesn't really think about anything when she's getting ready to race on the wall. She just focuses on doing the best she can. At the end of a tough-preliminary race Brittney had placed 11th. She swam a personal best time of 1:18.87! What Brittney didn't know is that the top 12 would advance to the finals.

"I really didn't think I made the finals, but I was so happy that I swam my personal best time in the backstroke," Brittney said.

Her brother Jon had senior night at his last home basketball game. There was a conflict because the family wanted her to be at Jon's senior night. So Brittney got showered and dressed and left right away. She made it to Jon's senior night and was able to enjoy her brother's half-time activities back at McNary High School.

On Saturday, the final for the varsity girls' 100 yard backstroke was getting closer to race time. No one knew where Brittney was.

"I was asking every girl, 'Where is Brittney?' No one seemed to know. Can someone please get on the phone and call Brittney!" Coach Phillips explained.

Brittney was home relaxing thinking her season was over. She received a call from one of the girls. They were ecstatic!

"I was really excited that I made the finals and didn't even realize it – so I hurried up to get to the Kroc Center – my parents got me there just in time," Brittney said.

Brittney swam a better time in the finals, placing 11th again, but the best part was that she outdid her previous time swimming a 1:16.85 – that made her day.

"She works very hard in the pool all season long. Sometimes Brittney is too hard on herself. It's easy for me to talk her out of the pressure she puts on herself. This young lady is an athlete that's very easy to coach. She wants to get better – you can see it. You get these girls now and then that are pleasers – Brittney is definitely a pleaser. She's always wearing a bubbly smile on her face," Coach Phillips said.

While swimming is possibly a college sport for her, she is also an outstanding bowler. Having one year of league bowling experience, Brittney entered a bowling tournament at Town and Country Lanes at the beginning of the 2013 school season. The Bowler of the Year Tournament included five boys. She would have a handicap of 80. Her first game she bowled a 233, second game a 246, and the third game a 253. Her total score was 732. She went on to win the tournament!

Scott and Tara have some advice for other parents that might have a daughter competing in swimming and striving to reach a goal like Brittney's.

"Encourage them but don't force them. Don't shove it down their throat. Don't tell them they can't do it. It's important that they not quit. If they make a commitment, they should finish what they started – very important," Scott said and Tara agreed.

There are things that no one knows about Brittney. I took pleasure to ask Scott this question.

"What someone might not know about Brittney is that she gets everything she wants. One year she wanted a car for

Christmas, she got it – I bought her hot wheels for a dollar. Another year she wanted a box of cat litter – we got it for her," Scott laughs.

Brittney will always remember the time her brother, Tim, drew on her body with permanent markers while she was sleeping. Her entire body was covered with sharpie colors – a masterpiece. When she woke up, no one really knows what went through her head.

Brittney has a great future ahead of her. This young girl has overcome so much in her early life. She still faces challenges ahead of her, but her willingness to not give up will take her a long way. We could see her swim on a college scholarship someday. She plans to add two weight-lifting classes to her training.

Her goal is to make it through college in Science or Health. She would love to eventually become a Nero-Ultrasound Technician.

Brittney, you are an inspiration to many young girls, keep it going young lady. You have a very bright future ahead of you.

Noah Torres, Nothing Stops this Legend from the Lake

Paul and Sophie Torres have five kids, Audra, Amanda, Angelica, Paul Jr., and the miracle kid, Noah (five years younger than Paul Jr.). Not too many families go through something with their youngest child like this family did. One summer I had the pleasure of traveling to Moses Lake, Washington. I enjoyed the visit and their hospitality in a big Spanish-looking home – beautiful design.

Their neighborhood was very quiet – not too many houses around. Sophie's parents lived next to them, but in-between the houses sat an acre of pasture. There weren't too many kids to play with, so the siblings relied on family games.

Noah's dad, Paul, was an outstanding baseball player all through high school. If he would have chosen to play college baseball, I'm certain that many colleges would have been interested. He now works for Inland Mechanical Construction as a Superintendent of Fabrication Construction – very skilled at his job.

Sophie played softball for several leagues in her younger days but that's about it other than watching her kids. She worked at American Foods for ten years, Takata

Inflation Systems for three years, and National Standards before becoming a homemaker.

Before sharing Noah's courageous story, it only seems fitting to acknowledge an incident that his mom, Sophie, was caught in unexpectedly. This happened a few years before Noah was born.

It was on a Friday in the year 1997 that Sophie's life would change. She would face such a hard time in her life – no one really expected this.

Paul was in Othello, Washington, finishing up a job that the company had assigned to him. He had taken a company truck and left his car parked at the shop outside of Moses Lake. He would be working later than expected and the office would be closed by the time he returned – he would not be able to get his paycheck.

"I remember Paul calling me and asking me if I could go pick up his check from his work. I was trying to decide whether to take our youngest child or leave him with the older kids. We were all hungry and I was getting ready to feed us – it was about 12:00 noon. I thought to myself, I can just go by myself and pick up some McDonald's burgers on the way back," Sophie said.

Paul Jr. was two years old at the time and was crying because he wanted to go with Sophie. Her oldest daughter, Audra, was there as well – she was always good about helping out her mom when she could.

"Mom, just leave him. He always cries when you leave and as soon as you're gone he stops crying," Audra said.

Sophie got into her van and as soon as she backed up she could see Paul Jr. looking out of the window crying. As difficult as that was for her, she started driving forward and arrived at Canterbury Lane and Wheeler Road. She was faced with a decision. Sophie could take highway 17 which would take her around the noon traffic in downtown Moses Lake, or she could drive through the downtown area which would get her to Paul's work site but at a much slower pace. Highway 17 is the road that leads to Ephrata, Washington.

"I decided to take Highway 17 to get there faster. I couldn't help but notice the beautiful sunny day we were having," Sophie said.

She arrived at the intersection of Highway 17 and Broadway Street. While she waited at the red light, Sophie noticed a whole string of cars behind her in the rear-view mirror. The light changed to green and she pressed the gas pedal to continue to her destination. She noticed an on-coming car with two teenagers arguing – a boy and a girl. The driver was veering head on at a high speed toward Sophie. Then she noticed the car would go back to the correct lane.
Sophie was approaching Parker Horn Bridge and a few thoughts went through her mind.

"I thought to myself in a glimpse, I could maybe stop and they would miss me, but I had a whole string of cars behind me. I could swerve to the right but I might go off the bridge. I started to hit my brakes but then noticed they had returned to their lane. I took a breath, then once again they started coming toward me out of control. I hit the brakes as hard as I could in hopes that they would miss me!" Sophie said.

Many things flashed through her mind as one could imagine if in that same position. She does remember one thing very clear that went through her mind.

"Oh God, please watch over my children if you decide to take me now. I closed my eyes not knowing if I was going to live or die," Sophie said.

Sophie was in a head-on collision that afternoon. She remembers waking up with the airbag plastered to her face and chest. The entire front of her car was smashed to the dash. When she woke up, she felt pain coming from her neck, chest, back, and her right foot. She also experienced severe headaches.

One of the other passengers from the on-coming car did not survive. A sixteen year-old girl died at the scene. The boy survived with a broken elbow and a few bumps and bruises.

There was a man that was looking at Sophie at the scene of the accident. He was one of the drivers among the traffic that stopped to help out.

"Are you okay? Don't worry, we've called the ambulance – on their way," he said.

When the paramedics arrived they had trouble getting Sophie out. Her van was pinned against the bridge rail.

"I was trying to not pass out. I was taught in CPR that if you bow your head between your legs this would prevent you from passing out. But the airbag was in the way and I could not do that. I heard the paramedic say, 'Where's your baby? There's a car seat in the back.' Thank God I left him at home," Sophie said.

After an hour and a half they were able to pull Sophie out by using a chainsaw to cut the door. She was on her way to the hospital emergency room.

Paul was coming back from Othello. He noticed the line of cars and the ambulance. He knew there was an accident – going through town instead of Highway 17 seemed to be the better choice. He finally made it home.

"Where's your mom?" Paul asked the kids.

He found out that she had been in an accident – a very bad one. Her parents had driven over to inform the kids. This was back in 1997 and there weren't any cell phones yet.

Sophie had suffered a concussion, broken ribs, and permanent damage to her foot. She had surgery (three pins inserted to her foot) and remained in bed for three months. When she started recovering she was given a special shoe to wear. Her foot was not working well. She had a limp that was very noticeable.

Her lawyer advised her to see a doctor in Seattle. He was one of the doctors that worked with the football team, the Seattle Seahawks. Doctor Pierce Scranton had the expertise to fix Sophie's foot and he would show her how to walk with a cane until then.

He wanted to be sure that she was not on certain medications, or pregnant, before performing the surgery to fix her foot. She had struggled for two years up to this point.

After the pregnancy test, the result showed positive. The surgery had to wait until after the baby was born, they would reconvene then. Sophie had to use a cane a few more months until she could have the surgery on her foot.

On September 14, 1999, Noah Torres was born at Samaritan Hospital, in Moses Lake, Washington. Paul and Sophie were excited to be bringing another boy into the family.

"When Noah was born, I remember looking at Paul, he was the whitest I'd ever seen him. Paul normally has very dark skin. He was looking at the baby with distress," Sophie said.

Noah was born with cleft lip, something the parents never would have imagined. After all, there weren't any previous generational family members with this condition that they knew of. It just didn't seem real that they would have yet something else to deal with.

The doctor reassured Paul and Sophie that things would be okay. He said it was fixable. Little Noah could have surgery in two months – the younger the better.

If the surgery isn't dealt with during the early years, the child could develop speech problems and other difficulties.

Cleft lip (cheiloschisis) is a physical split or separation of the two sides of the upper lip. A narrow opening or gap that is visible. It's an abnormal facial development during the carrying of the embryo. A statistic for this, 1 in 700 children are born with cleft lip or cleft palate every year. Clefts can also affect other parts of the face (eyes, ears, nose, cheeks, and forehead). In Noah's case it affected his lip and his nose.

"We were very happy to hear the news from the doctor. It was cleft lip and not cleft palate, where the roof of the mouth would have a hole and fewer teeth. That would have been more painful and more surgeries. Noah had cleft lip, which still required a process of surgeries throughout his young life," Sophie said.

Paul and Sophie cared so much for Noah that they would do anything to help him have a normal life. Noah would have seven surgeries throughout the years to fix the cleft lip he had.

It is a complicated process, because as Noah's body grew it affected things with his nose, and mouth. Plastic surgeries would be scheduled to fix the scar where the lip was split. Skin grafts would be taken to repair tissue, etc.

"We went to some conferences that had groups of people dealing with the same thing we were. They had kids with cleft lip or cleft palate. The sessions were very helpful to us," Sophie said.

Noah survived the first surgery and second. Before you knew it, he was running around as a four year-old kid. He was the youngest of the family and he became really close to Angelica, one of his sisters.

Paul never thought of enrolling Noah in any sports due to what could happen to him if he were to get hit – especially in baseball.

"I loved baseball and thought about my experiences getting hit by the baseball or getting run over at the base. That was the last thing I wanted Noah to go through. Our daughters played softball, and my oldest son played football and soccer. I didn't really pressure them to work harder at it – I just wanted them to have fun," Paul said.

Paul's dad never threw the baseball around with him when Paul was growing up. He claims that the older generation wasn't like that. The kids had to work at it on their own. With his kids, he would play with them and encourage them on whatever sport they wanted to pursue.

"The girls played softball in junior high school – good players but never got the chance to prove themselves because of politics. It was always tough for them because people knew who Paul was and how good he had been inside the diamond – a batting average of .300 - .500. He helped the Moses Lake Chiefs almost make it to the playoffs ending with a winning record. People would hear that the girls were Paul's daughters and they'd say things like, 'Your Paul's daughter you must be very good!' That put a little pressure on our daughters," Sophie said.

Noah had fire in his eyes and was around sports all the time. He watched his dad, sisters, and his older brother all the time.

On September 2003, his older sister Amanda locked the back door to prevent Noah from coming outside. She was going to work on her swing with the baseball bat. Amanda was a good hitter in softball – an average hitter in Moses Lake.

Noah was pretty darn short at the time as a four year-old kid. It was killing him not to be outside playing and learning from his sister. No one had guessed that this smart kid had figured out how to unlock the back door – accomplishing something at a very young age on his own.

"I had a softball tournament coming up and I hadn't practiced in days. I decided to go out to the backyard and swing the bat awhile. I didn't know Noah had followed me to the backyard. I locked the door, but he must have figured out how to unlock it," Amanda said.

Amanda started with a backward swing with full force. As she swung the bat, Noah was right behind her trying to say something to her. He stepped right into the strike zone. A loud sound came from the aluminum bat and Noah hit the ground unconsciously. Amanda started screaming as loud as she could – crying and talking to Noah.

Sophie was at her mom's house (an acre way), she had just got done helping with some painting. She had driven the van over and left the keys in the ignition.

"I heard the scream and saw Amanda and Noah on the ground in our backyard. I started running as fast as I could toward our house. I yelled at my mom to get my van and meet me in my driveway so we could take Noah to the doctor!" Sophie was ecstatic.

Noah was not responding at all, but he was throwing up. Sophie called Paul and he met them at Dr. Warner's clinic in Moses Lake. The doctor told them to take him to the emergency room at Samaritan Hospital right away.

"I felt horrible when that happened. I stayed with Noah talking to him and trying to get him to respond. I waited until Mom arrived to take him to the doctor," Amanda said.

It all happened so fast. Amanda felt really bad and was emotionally hurt. Her little brother was once again heading to the hospital.

He had suffered a severe concussion. After X-rays Noah was determined to have suffered a spider-fracture with at least three large cracks in his skull – roughly 12 total fractures.

"It was another nightmare – I was worried for my baby. Noah stayed the night and at 6:00 A.M. the doctor told us that since he had not awakened yet and he was a child, we needed to get him to Spokane. This hospital did not have the experience to treat children in Noah's condition. They were transferring him to Sacred Heart Children's Hospital in Spokane. One parent was allowed to ride in the helicopter. I went with him," Sophie said.

Paul picked up the other kids at home and drove to Spokane to meet Sophie and Noah there. The doctors weren't sure if Noah would make it there in time. It was scary that he could have ended up in a coma the rest of his life, or have had brain damage. They just didn't know.

They finally arrived at Sacred Heart Children's Hospital, in Spokane, Washington, he was immediately taken in. He remained in a coma for five days. One can't imagine the suffering this family went through and the uncertainty of what might happen.

"It was a very difficult situation for all of us – it was in God's hands," Sophie said in tears.

The accident happened on a Tuesday. Noah was in a coma until Saturday. He finally started responding and came out of the coma.

"Noah, do you remember what happened to you?" the doctor asked.

Everyone in the room was holding their breath – a dead silence.

"I got hit with a bat. I remember unlocking the door – I was just bored and wanted to play baseball," Noah said.

The relief that was felt was an amazing gift from God.

"He thought the doorknob was a baseball," Paul said laughing.

Noah almost died, but because of the quick response by his parents and the skilled medicine-field staff, he survived. Noah was a fighter and continues to be each day.

"I always knew Noah would be a special kid – always trying to keep up with the older kids no matter what they were doing," Sophie said.

The only thing on Noah's mind was getting back home. He did not want to be away from his family – he just wanted to go home.

Amanda has moved on and doesn't think about the accident anymore. She feels that things happen for a reason. It has made her and Noah stronger people.

"I was the next to the oldest kid and I watched my brothers and sisters for a long time. I was really close to Noah – I took care of him for many years. He was very forgiving and understood that it was an accident. From that experience, I have learned that you have to be more careful around kids. I now have a daughter, Brooklyn. It has changed me in a way that I want to keep her safe – always paying close attention to her," Amanda said.

Angelica was the daughter always looking after him once Amanda got married. Those two became really close. She spent a lot of time with Noah.

Noah started showing interest in baseball – he wanted to play baseball, but his parents were not too thrilled about the idea.

"When you watch older kids, you think that you're at their level. You want to be like them – as good as them. I want my kids to be good. I want them to be like me. With sports you can do many great things. My parents grew up working in the fields – that was a different life that I don't want for my kids. I never pushed my kids to do sports and I never planned on Noah playing any kind of sport because of what he went through," Paul said.

Noah attended Lake View Elementary School, Garden Heights Elementary School, and Chief Moses Middle School. It was uncomfortable for him at times because of kids that would repeatedly ask him what was wrong with his lip.

Noah felt like kids had their little groups. He could connect with some kids but it was always tough for him to be part of a small group. Was he annoying to the other kids at times? Was he that different that his peers didn't accept him in their little groups? We really don't have an answer to that. I do know that kids can be cruel at times – that's just reality.

Noah worked by himself when it came to projects or everyday stuff. He felt more comfortable that way. When he played sports with other kids, Noah connected a lot better than just at a school playground or in class.

"They would always bug me by asking, 'What's that?' I got tired of them doing that. Sometimes I just thought to myself, 'Why did I have to be born with a cleft lip?' It just wasn't fair. I've learned that God made me this way for a reason. I'm choosing to become as successful as I can be," Noah said.

Noah has always been a leader type of kid. He was always doing well academically maintaining a 3.4 GPA. He was also involved with Boy Scouts. This young boy was always the type of kid that was disciplining other kids – explaining to them about safety or what they should be doing to be in good behavior.

Noah has won the Grant County Spelling Bee Contest two years in a row. That takes some doing.

"I'm not ashamed to say that we offer Noah $100.00 if he gets straight As. That motivates him a little to do his best," Sophie laughs.

A sense of humor is an understatement. He was always making other kids laugh. There was a teacher in school that had a serious attitude. Noah's goal for the year was to get a smile out of her.

"He had a great sense of humor and had tried to make me laugh all year long. Well he finally did," Mrs. Ford told Sophie.

Noah had good friends he hung out with at times. August Johnson was one of his friends but he ended up moving to Idaho. Coltin Morrison was another best friend.

"Coltin and I were best buddies – we both had medical problems like headaches all the time. We would always ask each other, 'So how many days did you miss last week?' We had a lot of things in common – we could relate to each other," Noah said.

Caleb Juarez was another good friend he had. Caleb was a baseball teammate he practiced with and hung out with during baseball season.

Noah worked through the headaches, some days were better than others. It's difficult for a young kid to start school and get adjusted to new kids, classes and teachers. But to include what Noah was going through must have been very challenging for this young man.

To have a positive outlook in life like he did was inspiring to many people. Noah played baseball and basketball. Football would be out of the question due to his head and what could possibly happen if he were to bang helmets with another player.

Paul and Sophie never expected Noah to do sports, but they knew that it was only a matter of time before he asked them. One day he came home after school and he looked at his mom. He had saved enough money up on his own to pay for the baseball-league fee. It was too tough to prevent their son from doing what he really loved and begged for.

Noah liked paying for his own way. He mowed his grandparents' lawn – a fairly large one. They paid him to do that. He also mowed his backyard lawn which is about an eighth of an acre. He does odd jobs around the house. He saves his money for sports jerseys and sign-up fees.

"I remember that day he came up to me and asked me to take him to sign up for a baseball team. I thought to myself, 'Oh my God.' It's what he really wanted to do," Sophie said.

That day Sophie talked to Paul about the matter ... they both agreed to allow him. Sophie took Noah to sign up for the Cal Ripkin Little League. Noah was ten years old when he started playing organized baseball. His dad worked with him with a few baseball skills but not as much as we might think.

"I was worried for Noah. The thought of him getting hit by the baseball was mind boggling. He was learning to be a pitcher – all I thought about was what if a strong kid hits the ball right at him? Those baseballs go seventy to eighty miles an hour sometimes," Paul said.

His dad started realizing that Noah was not going to take no for an answer. He wanted to become a great baseball player. He realized he had a late start, but with hard work and persistence, he would one day catch up with the other kids.

"My dad inspired me to start playing baseball, I watched him play many years. I wanted to be as good as he was. I also watched a lot of major league baseball on TV with my dad. I just learned to love the game," Noah said.

Paul had a nephew who played college baseball for Columbia Basin Community College in the Tri-Cities area. He helped his team win the championship title. He learned the correct technique and was very knowledgeable about the way the game is played today.

Paul would have his nephew, Rigo Castillo, work with Noah and instruct him on how to hit, pitch, slide, catch, and many other skills.

"I wanted Noah to learn the right way. I was a pretty good baseball player, but I learned from just watching other great baseball players. My dad never worked with me or took me for baseball lessons. I wanted Noah to have the right training. I couldn't think of anyone better than Rigo," Paul said.

Noah played for the Cardinals when he was ten years old. When he was eleven, he played for the Marlins and at twelve for the Mariners. These were names of teams in a city little league. His best year so far had been with the Mariners. His batting average was anywhere from .200 to .300 estimated. That's not too bad for a kid that overcame so many obstacles in his early life.

There was a time when his dad was coaching the all-star team at the end of the season. Noah had made the all-star team! The Nationals were playing in Wenatchee, Washington.

Noah was a pretty good pitcher, but he was still learning. The team they were playing was very tough and Paul knew in the back of his head that his team didn't have a chance to win. He had to select one of his players to pitch in the final innings.

"I knew my son would be upset at me. First, I was thinking of his safety. Then I thought about how a lot of dads out there favor their kids. But most important, I was thinking of what it would do to my son emotionally. He would get the blame for the loss – I just couldn't take that chance with what he had been through as a young kid – I cared too much for him," Paul said.

Paul put his pride aside and focused on his son's well-being. A tough decision, especially when the people sitting on bleachers were questioning his decision. Why would he not let his own kid pitch?

"I wanted to pitch that game so bad. It was hard for me to not be out there. I wanted that to be my decision. I figured if I got hit by the baseball, or if I lost the game for us, I would take that fall, I had done it before – it wasn't any different," Noah said.

"He amazed us so many times – he would always get hits and make it to base. He's always played at his level never played up with the older kids. His batting had improved every year he played," Sophie said.

One of Paul's favorite memories of Noah playing baseball was when he was playing shortstop during an all-star game. A line drive came to Noah – he caught it and made a heads-up play to get a player out. Sophie's favorite memory was when he hit his first home run.

At the end of the baseball season, Noah received a baseball trophy. It was his first baseball trophy he had been awarded.

Noah has become a multi-sport athlete. He is playing a lot of basketball these days, he wants to improve his defense, shooting and dribbling skills. He's not afraid to play one-one-one with anyone – he plays against his dad now and then.

"It bothered me when I played certain kids that had a bad attitude. We'd play one-on-one in basketball. I would get beat pretty bad – I could take that. One kid in particular would rub it in my face after he won the game. What he didn't realize is that he had been playing since he was four years old. I started playing when I was ten. I'm working hard to get better every day – I got plenty of time to catch up," Noah said.

Noah plans to attend basketball camps in the summer and at times ask his brother-in-law, Bryan McCaffery, who is Amanda's husband, to work with him. Bryan is a basketball coach for Moses Lake Secondary School. The school is similar to an alternative school. He knows the game well and definitely can help Noah with some skills and share his basketball knowledge.

In the summers Noah plans to attend the Matt Espinoza Royal Scot Hoop Camp. This camp is one of the best in Salem, Oregon. Kids of all ages learn some of the best basketball skills – ball handling, defense, shooting, etc. Matt makes it a fun camp for everyone – girls and boys.

Noah has found a liking to the state of Oregon. He's chosen to try some basketball camps there. He also travels to visit relatives that live there.

"I love Oregon, it's a great place – that's the number one place I'd want to spend my birthday at," Noah said smiling.

Not only did Noah play baseball and basketball, but he also loved bowling. He watched his parents bowl as a youngster, and showed interest. Bowling is a much safer sport.

"We signed him up for bowling lessons. Every Saturday morning Paul and I would look at each other. Who's going to take him ... me or you? It's something we both knew was important to Noah. We supported him on this, but at the same time we enjoyed sleeping in on Saturdays," Sophie laughs.

Once again, his dad was a good bowler, but didn't have the time to show him skills. He had some of the guys from the bowling alley show him some techniques. It was only a matter of time until Noah developed a solid game.

Noah has won eight trophies in bowling tournaments including the city championship for his age group. His best score as a twelve year-old kid was 198 – his average is 149. Not too bad for the youngster. He's determined to be great at anything he does.

He took second place in the PPK (Punt, Pass, and Kick) Contest and he's won a Hotshot Basketball Competition.

Hotshot shooting is a contest in which a kid shoots baskets from several designated spots on the basketball court. The objective is to make as many as you can in one minute – the time may vary at different competitions.

His brother Paul gets mad sometimes when Noah actually beats him at a game of "horse" or in a game of bowling. But he supports his brother and cares for him. His sisters all support him as well and want him to succeed in whatever he does.

"I get jealous sometimes because he does some things better than I do, but I'm very happy for him and I want him to continue getting better at everything," Paul Jr. said.

Paul Jr. has been around Noah just about every day. He definitely has a brotherly-love relationship with him. They get into arguments and battles like any brothers do. But they both enjoy talking sports, competing in bowling and basketball. It's a great combination to have.

Noah seems to be closer to his mom when it comes to asking serious questions. In the sports world of course he's closer to his dad. His dad was always working and for years was not around the family that much. If he wasn't working he was playing in a softball tournament or basketball tournament – hanging out with his friends. He did his best to find time to be around his family.

Sophie was home all the time and she spent a lot time with Noah – they were really close and for Noah it was easy to ask her anything.

"When I was in fourth grade kids were spreading rumors that you could get pregnant by French kissing. One of my friends asked me if that was true. That day I went home and asked my mom if it was true. She slapped me and I went to my room crying. I decided that if I had children someday in the future I would never do that to them. I talked to my children at a very early age and told them they could ask me anything they wanted – I have an open communication with all my children," Sophie said.

Noah worked hard at getting better with his pitching skills. At his house he drew a box on the shed. This box would be the same height as a strike zone. He practiced everyday to hit that target consistently. He worked on his footing and his arm technique. Releasing the baseball the correct way is important in baseball.

"It has to come from the heart. I want to go out and prove a lot of people wrong. Because of the way I was born and some of the things I've dealt with in life so young, some people probably doubt I'll ever be good enough. I want to go somewhere after high school. I want to play in college, and possibly in the pros some day. I'll focus on baseball or basketball. I like Oregon State University, or possibly Washington State. I'd love to go to high school in Mount Vernon, where my sister Angelica lives. It's close to Seattle where there could be scouts," Noah said.

"One thing about Noah is that he listens well to his coaches. He's very easy to coach. If he ever had a complaint or something, he would always talk to the coach afterward away from everyone else. It's relaxing to know that he's determined to succeed in something – he's trying all of his options. We're very proud of Noah," Paul said.

Noah's parents have some advice for other parents that might have a son or a daughter dealing with a same situation.

"Love them, help them out and support them," Sophie said.

"Sometimes you have to push them a little – they have to work at it. They aren't going anywhere lying on the couch watching TV," Paul said.

Noah Torres is a miracle kid and a legend from Moses Lake. He has had seven surgeries to this day. He says the surgeries don't bother him, it's the liquid diet he has to go on afterward that bothers him.

"I think of those surgeries as sports injuries and that makes me feel better about them. I think positive – how it's going to make me a stronger person," Noah said.

Noah loves baseball during baseball season, and he loves basketball during basketball season. He would love to play college baseball or basketball someday. And we can't rule out the Pro Bowler's Tour someday – we'll just have to see.

Something people might not know about Noah is that he's really close to the Lord. He reads his Bible regularly. He likes keeping that part between him and God. He'll be the first to admit, now at fourteen years old, that he's always learning a lot every day.

"Anything can happen with the power of God. I like this verse from the Bible. Matthew 19:26 – But Jesus looked at them and said, 'With man this is impossible, but with God all things are possible.' I'm a firm believer in that," Noah said.

I have no doubt that his young man will be successful in whatever he decides to do. With the Lord next to him, his parents supporting him and his sisters and brother on his side ... this can only help him continue his quest. Great job Noah, never give up, you are amazing!

Credits

Front cover photos were taken by David Espinoza except for Ball Up photos and Brittney Kiser (taken by Hanna Russell).

CEO Demetrious Spencer for permission to use the Ball Up Streetball photos

Weiss family for Janelle photos inside book.

Hurlburt family for Alex photos inside book

Chuhlantseff family for Brooke photos inside book

Brattain family for Daniel photos inside book

Kiser family for Brittney photos inside book

Torres family for Noah photos inside book

Craig Huston Photography for Alex uniform photos inside book

Kim Phillips for Brittney swim meet photo inside book

Matt Espinoza for the back cover photo, except Brooke photo by David Espinoza

Sources

Most of the material that I have written comes from countless hours of interview time with athletes and their parents. The families interviewed were the Boucher family; Weiss family; Hurlburt family; Holmes family; Chuhlantseff family; Brattain family; Kiser family and Torres family.

Page 16   "Hip dysplasia" *Wikipedia: The Free Encyclopedia.* Wikimedia Foundation, Inc. 22 July 2004 Web 29 Oct. 2013 <http://en.wikipedia.org/wiki/Hip_dysplasia>

Pages 30-47   "Streetball" Season Two, The And 1 Mixtape Tour, copyright 2004 And 1 Entertainment

Page 53   "Malaria" Centers of Disease Control and Prevention, high level information, <http://www.cdc.gov/malaria/about/faqs.html>

Page 79   "Amniotic band constriction" *Wikipedia: The Free Encyclopedia.* Wikimedia Foundation, Inc. 22 July 2004 Web 29 Oct. 2013 <http://en.wikipedia.org/wiki/Amniotic_band_constriction>

Page 143 "Cerebral hemorrhage" *Wikipedia: The Free Encyclopedia.* Wikimedia Foundation, Inc. 22 July 2004 Web 29 Oct. 2013 <http://en.wikipedia.org/wiki/Cerebral_hemorrhage>

Page 170 "Nike Border Clash" <http://nikeborderclash.runnerspace.com/eprofile.php>

Page 197 "Backstroke" *Wikipedia: The Free Encyclopedia.* Wikimedia Foundation, Inc. 22 July 2004 Web 29 Oct. 2013 <http://en.wikipedia.org/wiki/Backstroke>

Page 200 "Dyslexia" *Wikipedia: The Free Encyclopedia.* Wikimedia Foundation, Inc. 22 July 2004 Web 29 Oct. 2013 <http://en.wikipedia.org/wiki/Dyslexia>

Page 201 4T-Trail: Blogspot, the description of the 4T-Trail, http://4t-trail.org

Page 215 "Cleft lip" *Wikipedia: The Free Encyclopedia.* Wikimedia Foundation, Inc. 22 July 2004 Web 29 Oct. 2013 <http://en.wikipedia.org/wiki/Cleft_lip_and_palate>